MICHEL FOUCAULT AND
THE GAMES OF TRUTH

Michel Foucault and the Games of Truth

Herman Nilson

Translated by Rachel Clark

First published in Great Britain 1998 by
MACMILLAN PRESS LTD
Houndmills, Basingstoke, Hampshire RG21 6XS and London
Companies and representatives throughout the world

A catalogue record for this book is available from the British Library.

ISBN 0–333–69232–2

 First published in the United States of America 1998 by
ST. MARTIN'S PRESS, INC.,
Scholarly and Reference Division,
175 Fifth Avenue, New York, N.Y. 10010

ISBN 0–312–21297–6

Library of Congress Cataloging-in-Publication Data
Nilson, Herman, 1965–
Michel Foucault and the games of truth / Herman Nilson ;
translated by Rachel Clark.
p. cm.
Translated from the German.
Includes bibliographical references and index.
ISBN 0–312–21297–6
1. Foucault, Michel—Contributions in philosophy of life.
2. Nietzsche, Friedrich Wilhelm, 1844–1900—Influence. 3. Foucault,
Michel. Histoire de la sexualité. 4. Sex customs—History.
5. Ethics, Ancient. 6. Life. I. Title.
B2430.F724N55 1998
194—dc21   97–38831
                                                              CIP

This book is printed on paper suitable for recycling and made from fully managed and
sustained forest sources.

10   9   8   7   6   5   4   3   2   1
07 06 05 04 03 02 01 00 99 98

Printed and bound in Great Britain by
Antony Rowe Ltd, Chippenham, Wiltshire

To Thomas – Ecce Amicus!

Contents

Acknowledgements

Firstly I have to thank Rachel Clark for her meticulous translation of the German manuscript and the countless hours of discussion. Without her contribution the English version would have been beyond reach.

I would like to thank both Professor Norbert Bolz, whose seminar at Berlin's Free University in April 1988 sparked off the idea for this book, and Professor Dietmar Kamper, for his support during the writing of the doctoral thesis.

Furthermore I would like to express my thanks to the Studienwerk Villigst for their financial assistance, enabling me to pursue research at the Bibliothèque du Saulchoir (Paris) and at the British Library (London). Thanks also to all those who gave their encouragement: Stephanie Kunze for her help and hospitality during my stay in England, Bo Isenberg for his productive criticism, Nathaniel Carin for his invaluable suggestions during the final reworking of the text, Daniel Defert for his informative insight into the cynical part of Foucault's philosophy.

List of Abbreviations

AK   *The Archaeology of Knowledge*, trans. A. M. Sheridan Smith. London, 1972.

BSH Dreyfus, Hubert Lederer and Rabinow, Paul: *Beyond Structuralism and Hermeneutics*. Chicago, 1982.

CA   'Qu'est-ce que la critique? [Critique et Aufklärung]' (In: *Bulletin de la Société française de philosophie*, 84 (2). April-June, pp. 35-63.

CS   *The History of Sexuality: The Care of the Self*, trans. Robert Hurley. London, 1990.

DE   *Dits et Écrits*. 1954–88 (Bibliothèque des Sciences humaines). 4 Volumes. Édition établie sous la direction de Daniel Defert et François Ewald avec la collaboration de Jacques Lagrange. Paris, 1994.

DT   *Discourse and Truth: The Problematization of Parrhesia*, transcript of six lectures in English. Joseph Pearson (ed.). Evanston, 1985.

FR   Rabinow, Paul (ed.): *The Foucault Reader*. New York, 1984.

HS   *The History of Sexuality: An Introduction*, trans. Robert Hurley. Harmondsworth, 1978.

TS   'Technologies of the Self'. In: *Technologies of the Self: A Seminar with Michel Foucault*. Luther H. Martin, Huck Gutman, Patrick H. Hutton (eds.). Amherst, Mass., 1988, pp. 16–49.

UP   *The History of Sexuality: The Use of Pleasure*, trans. Robert Hurley. London, 1992.

Nietzsche is quoted with volume/page number according to the German edition of his complete works (*Kritische Studienausgabe*. dtv, de Gruyter. München, Berlin, New York, 1980). Where Foucault and Nietzsche are quoted, this book mainly refers to the original French and German texts.

Introduction

The attempts to approach Michel Foucault's thought and interpret his works under various aspects are numerous and by no means mere objects of philosophical debate. This interdisciplinary 'confusion' on the writings Foucault left to posterity should be seen, however, not as a disadvantage, but as the result of Foucault's own efforts. Nonetheless, his studies lead to the core of philosophical questioning: to the analysis of the games of truth. In this, Foucault did not view philosophy as an abstract care of the truth, but biographically as 'an "ascesis", *askēsis*, an exercise of oneself in the activity of thought' (UP 9).

It is neither a question of indicating the latest developments in research on Foucault, nor of formulating the many-faceted, heterogeneous work as a uniform *oeuvre*. If Foucault's work can be seen as 'uniform', however, it is as an ongoing genealogical project; a project which did not aim at presenting a 'theory of power', but at reintroducing the problem of the subject – to the point of problematizing the sovereign moral subject in antiquity which Foucault described in his final books. In these final studies on an aesthetics and ethics of existence in self-relation it becomes particularly clear how much Foucault's thought was indebted to Nietzsche's preparatory work.

The following study is not intended simply as yet another contribution to the extensive secondary literature on Foucault's work; rather, it is the attempt to experience through Foucault Nietzsche's ethical 'weight' and hence the cultural conditions for a stylistics of existence by the example of the ancient dictum of self-care (heautocratism). Such a culture of the self is not reserved for those athletes of the intellect, the philosophers, but is open to all those individuals who are willing to care for themselves as possibly the most important item. This self-concern should not be misconstrued as a narcissistic, vain self-contemplation, but as the condition for a lifelong philosophical exercise with the aesthetic aim of a transformation of the self.

Consequently, self-care is also constitutive for Foucault's own work and is revealed, for example, in that unmistakeable form of a self-staging which is not polemically addressed at potential critics, but recurs programmatically in his entire lifework. This self-staging is also seen as a warning against hasty 'scientific' conclusions regarding his work, which Foucault wished to be viewed first and foremost as analyses of specific games of truth. In his inaugural lecture at the Collège de France, Foucault had already made clear his wish 'to be carried beyond all possible beginnings ... I would like to have been aware that at the moment of speaking a nameless voice had preceded me for a long time ... and instead of being the one from whom the discourse flowed I would be rather in the mercy of its flow, a tiny gap, the point of its possible disappearance'.[1] In other words, 'no, no, I'm not where you are lying in wait for me, but over here, laughing at you' (AK 17). In a newspaper interview ten years after his inaugural lecture, the 'philosophe masqué' expressed himself in a similar manner: He would like to remain unrecognized, anonymous (cf. DE 4/104–10).[2] In his final work, *The History of Sexuality*, Foucault also remained true to himself: 'There are times in life when the question of knowing if one can think differently than one thinks ... is absolutely necessary if one is to go on ... reflecting at all' (UP 8).

In the place of a theorization, this study will highlight Foucault's motives and strategies in order to reveal the attitudes, the ethos of a thinker for whom scientific work did not begin with the 'object of research', but in the 'critical work that thought brings to bear on itself'. For Foucault it was here that began the permanent challenge to attain enlightenment of oneself and thus a greater maturity; a challenge which is the task of each and every individual, at any time. In a Nietzschean sense, philosophy should be seen as a 'gay science', which, starting from the problematization of contemporary processes, invents new possibilities of thought and action – thus philosophy should be 'the assay or test by which, in the game of truth, one undergoes changes' (UP 9).

This study is comprised of two parts: In the first part the most important aspects of ancient aesthetics and ethics of existence in self-relation are reiterated based on a textual analysis of the second and third volumes of *The History of Sexuality*. This will illustrate Foucault's attempt to make parts of ancient moral reflection available to a modern post-Christian experience, thus explaining and paying tribute to Nietzsche's admiration of Greek culture. This is not a question of a nostalgic 'return to the Greeks' as the effort to overcome the ever-present Christian *Weltanschauung* and order of values; it is rather concerned with a reproblematization of ancient self-technologies as an opportunity to give one's individual life a form which, because it is reflexive, necessarily includes one's own transformation. This textual analysis of Foucault's later work precedes the actual interpretation and serves to illustrate the physiological facts which forestall every philosophy. It summarizes Foucault's most important points of ancient moral reflection, and guides those readers less familiar with Foucault's final work towards a better understanding of its aesthetical and ethical implications which can be traced back to Nietzsche.

The second part, instead of premising a 'theoretical unity' in his work, outlines Foucault's philosophical ethos and shows the extent to which philosophy is a question of critical attitude. This preconditions that it no longer be looked upon as a science, but as an exercise in thought and a stylistics of existence whose permanent challenge is freedom as a work of 'désassujettissement' (de-subjugation) (CA 39). Here Kant's reply to the question 'What is Enlightenment?' and Nietzsche's self-stylization as demanded in his aphorism 'One thing is needful', form two central aspects of Foucault's thought. By concluding with Nietzsche's physiological objections, this study establishes the connection to the pagan stylistics of existence as thematized in *The History of Sexuality,* and reveals the topicality of Nietzsche, visible in all of Foucault's books:[3] the need for self-care after God's death.

Part I:
Pagan Self-Technologies

'… in its lack of self-control,
in that which the Romans call impotentia,
modern personality betrays its weakness.'

(Friedrich Nietzsche, 1/285)

1

The Art of Temperance

DIFFERENT PERSPECTIVES

Foucault's primary interest in a history of sexuality as experience was the genealogical reconstruction of the hermeneutical subject of desire, that is to show why we reveal ourselves today as desiring subjects. After the preceding discourse analysis and an analysis of power reminiscent of the first volume of *The History of Sexuality*, Foucault turns his attention to the technologies of the self, 'to study the games of truth in the relationship of self with self and the forming of oneself as a subject' (UP 6).

According to his original plan, Foucault placed his studies of a history of sexuality in the time between the sixteenth and nineteenth centuries. An alteration became necessary when he gave his project a new direction with a fundamental question which went beyond any previous historical studies. 'Why had we turned sexuality into a moral experience?' (DE 4/705). This extension of his research interest caused him to go further back to early Christian moral history, and ultimately to Greek antiquity of the fifth and fourth centuries BC.[1]

In the following, a detailed textual analysis is used to highlight the most important aspects of pagan ethics examined by Foucault. This analysis is intended to prepare the way for a later definition of the 'culture of the self' which is central to this work, and indicate the current problem to which Foucault's studies on Greek antiquity are dedicated.

In order to cast an impartial glance at the moral experience of antiquity, and to avoid conventional conceptions – i.e. without applying a 'modern standard' – Foucault placed new terminological accents so as to reproduce as vividly as possible that which could be designated 'ancient ethos'. For this he made a selection of classical texts which reflected specific exposition of problems within ancient Greek morality, and which were attributed with an 'etho-poetic' (UP 13) function. With this Foucault specified the kind

3

of approach to these texts, which were not to be functionalized as objects of a hermeneutical subject-decoding, but should be viewed in a more sober light for what they were: 'practical texts', a 'framework of everyday conduct' (UP 12–13).

For Foucault, this distancing from a hermeneutics of the subject was important for two reasons: It is a definitive rejection of those 'confessional procedures',[2] ranging from the Christian confessional through to the 'talking cure' prescribed by psychoanalysis, which try to discover the 'truth' about the 'subject'. At the same time the etho-poetical, non-hermeneutical interpretation of the classical texts reflects Foucault's attitude towards his own work: He wished to see his own studies understood as the thought, not the knowledge of a transformation and stylization of the self. As a consequence of this differentiation, which expresses not least its doubts about academic self-perception, Foucault was often accused of not exercising enough care in the selection of the Greek texts. For the genealogist, however, it was not so much a question of the sources, which were in part uncertain anyway, at least as far as their authorship, and sometimes also their chronological order was concerned; he was more interested in the practices of a self-constitution expounded in them.

By defining the ancient texts on ethics as 'etho-poetic', Foucault was making clear that the texts were not written with the intention of approaching a theory on the basics of ethics. Instead, it was a question of practical books with certain prescriptions and exercises which one should read, 'to reread, to meditate upon, to learn, in order to construct a lasting matrix for one's own behavior' (DT 97). In a more comprehensive sense, Foucault also saw this as the task of philosophy: not to devise some theory on ethics or the subject, but to provide a basic structure for the formulation of individual conduct.

In his analysis Foucault directed himself towards those ethical aspects which were of central significance for life in antiquity, and through which the self-constitution of the moral subject could be exemplified: The body with regard to dietetics and the use of its pleasures; the institution of marriage and its economics for the management of home and household; the relationships between men with their central concern for the love of boys; and finally wisdom, philosophy itself, which leads Foucault to the core of his ethical reflections.

Foucault expressly drew attention to the fact that in ancient

Greece there predominated a morality oriented towards the needs of the man. This sort of moral reflection 'was an elaboration of masculine conduct carried out from the viewpoint of men in order to give form to *their* behavior' (UP 22–3). This reference to male morality in antiquity is not without significance for the approach to Foucault's final works, and already anticipates an initial criticism. Especially in feminist circles, there was repeated criticism that Foucault ignored the role of the woman.[3] Foucault's question regarding the constitution of the relationship to oneself excludes, at least for his analysis of antiquity, the monogamous relationship between man and woman which was only institutionalized and ideologically consolidated in the later Stoa and early Christian periods. Foucault was not interested in the forms of woman's subordination in ancient society, let alone did he want to pursue, with a modern, emancipated standard, a criticism of male-dominated society in the ancient world. For him another aspect of ancient male morality was decisive: The 'monosexual' social structure through which a culture of the self was given its specific basis. In this respect the notorious points of view on the modern 'battle of the sexes' were unimportant for Foucault and his analysis of self-relations. Instead he referred to Lillian Faderman's book, *Surpassing the Love of Men*, published 1980, in which the aspect of monosexuality is thematized for the female side as well.[4]

Furthermore, Foucault did not aspire to any 'theory of the subject': 'And since no Greek thinker ever found a definition for the subject, never looked for one, I would simply say that there is no subject ... in classical antiquity a problematization of the constitution of the self as subject is missing'[5] (DE 4/706). The word subject, nevertheless employed, is a technical term whose meaning arises from the ethical-moral context analysed by Foucault. Neither was Foucault concerned with a subject defined transcendentally or otherwise metaphysically, whose origin or finality was to be looked for; but rather with a male individual as a free citizen within the order of the city, which he, as free citizen, had to serve. This basic political prerequisite did not pursue the altruistic aim of sacrificing oneself to the common good, but rather, 'as the elaboration and stylization of an activity in the exercise of its power and the practice of its liberty' (UP 23).

For the definition of the individual as a self-constituting moral subject, and for a closer definition of his use of the term 'subject', Foucault introduced the phrase *ethical substance* (UP 26).[6] In the example of the 'etho-poetic' function of the texts, Foucault had already attempted to make clear that with this term he was declaring himself to be against all form of an enigmatic self which would merely have to be discovered. The definition of the ethical substance arises from 'the way in which the individual has to constitute this or that part of himself as the prime material of his moral conduct' (UP 26).

For Foucault a further characteristic of self-constitution in antiquity was also decisive: The ancient subject is diametrically opposed to the legal one. Gearing one's behaviour to norms and laws was not relevant for the development of one own's conduct; relevant was the very distance from exterior, institutional constraints. Here there is a difference to the modern subject which was decisive for Foucault with regards to moral self-constitution and self-technologies. In antiquity, the subject constituted himself within the given unity of reason (*logos*) and body, beyond institutional power and state legal systems.

The basic prerequisite for the fashioning of an individual's ethical substance is the maturity conveyed by the logos. This however, is not primarily constitutive for the work of enlightenment or – as Max Weber would say – for the 'disenchantment'[7] (*Entzauberung*) of the world, but is crucial for leading a beautiful life. This maturity, which was useful to the individual himself and without obligation to a system or an institution, was the basis upon which Foucault unfolded the type of problematization which determined the life of the free man. In this context he considered the 'ethical work' and the 'teleology of the moral subject' which also outline the problem of a correct lifestyle: How do I deal with my pleasures in order to be master, and not slave of myself in relation to those pleasures? What use must I make of my life for it to be beautiful and, what is more, for it to retain its lustre for others after my own death?

At this point it is already clear that Foucault's final studies no longer pursued the development of a critique of discourse practices (By which discourse did psychiatry seize madness as an object of research?), or institutions (How did prison develop into a constitutive instrument of state power practice?), but the revelation of a person's fundamental option: making oneself the starting point of a work on oneself. '*It is that*, which I wanted to reconstruct: the fashioning and the development of a practice of the self, whose objective was to constitute oneself as the worker on the beauty of one's own life' (DE 4/671).

THE PLEASURES AS ETHICAL SUBSTANCE

In order to introduce into his studies that change in perspective which had led him to the Greeks, Foucault had to free himself from the conventional terminology; that is, from that knowledge already accepted as common knowledge, so that the reader's view was also opened onto a subject transposed beyond modern concepts and theories.[8] To this belonged above all the massive terminological apparatus of psychoanalysis, which Foucault criticized as the aggravated Christian compulsion to confess.[9]

The first term which requires clarification is that of 'sexuality', which Foucault interpreted as an invention of the nineteenth century. The Greeks possessed a less charged concept of sex and sexuality. Instead, they preferred 'a nominalized adjective: *ta aphrodisia* ... 'Things' or 'pleasures of love' (UP 35). Their conception of 'sex' was of a more elementary kind: It contained the relation of the body to its pleasures, the flesh to its needs. For them, the permanent questioning as to the truth of the desire, which for Foucault seemed symptomatic of the present day, was of secondary importance.

The term *aphrodisia* is by no means an equivalent to the modern concept of sexuality. Foucault did not, therefore, give an adequate translation. This is also connected with the different evaluations attached to terms in their respective historical context. Above all, it is connected to the type of time-related problematizations which form around concepts, necessitating a different approach. For some essential findings Foucault had the English historian Kenneth J. Dover to thank. Regarding the uncertain definition of the term *aphrodisia*, Foucault referred to Dover's book *Greek Homosexuality*[10] which also moved away from the stereotypical conception of homosexuality in particular, and sexuality in general.

For a closer definition Foucault introduced along with *aphrodisia* three other Greek terms which problematized the field of sexual behaviour: For moral reflection stands the term *chrēsis* as 'type of subjection' (UP 37), which defines the use of the pleasures; the term *enkrateia* reflects the kind of control necessary for constituting a moral subject of oneself; and the term *sōphrosynē*, relating to moderation or wisdom as a teleological principle of the individual. Foucault's ethical quadrangle for the interpretation of ancient moral experience condenses itself in this way into an ontology, deontology, ascetics and finally teleology.

Foucault by no means intended these terms to lay the foundation for a 'theory of the subject'. They serve rather as tools[11] which should allow important areas of ancient moral experience to be brought to light. They reflect the manner of experience at a time when the absence of large institutions opened up another approach to sexual desires, and therefore to oneself. Foucault's analysis of *aphrodisia* neither shrouds a 'glittering sexual array' (HS 72), nor is it concerned with a classification or decipherment of desire.

There were no laws or rigid rules which prescribed to the Greeks how they should 'correctly' behave with regard to 'sexuality'. Nevertheless, retaining reserve towards the pleasures accorded was a peculiarity of ancient moral reflection. The Greeks viewed the pleasures with a severity, a didactic care, which did not aim at giving them a legal form, but at setting limits to the power of their rebellion in favour of a virile self-control. In contrast to Christian morality of the sinfulness of the sexual drive and of the flesh, which, through ceaseless self-purification, should both be forced back to the darkness of their origin, in ancient Greece the *aphrodisia* occasioned a moderating stance to be adopted with regards to pleasures.

For the Greeks, the symptomatic of *Verdrängung* (repression) later diagnosed by Freudian psychoanalysis, was the scene of an ethical activity and concern, a method of dealing with pleasures. Neither was the form of the pleasures made into the problem, but 'the activity they manifested. Their dynamics was much more important than their morphology' (UP 42). Where later the 'poly-morph perverse' steps onto the stage of modernity's obsession with the significance of sexuality, the Greek was simply a man who had sexual intercourse (*aphrodisiazein*). Furthermore, in ancient Greek perception of morality there was not yet a differentiation between act, desire and pleasure, notwithstanding the variety of preferences or the intensity of the pleasures. The *aphrodisia* were reflected in their entirety as an ethical problem. The care of one's sexual lifestyle was not expressed in a theoretical division of single elements of *aphrodisia*, but precisely in experiencing their unity in one's life.

Not an ontology of lack, but one of strength as a quantitative size dominated the reflection on pleasures. With this strength it was essential to maintain moderation in dealing with both women and with boys. The strength of the *aphrodisia* only became problematic

at the moment of immoderation, when one subjugated oneself to
the pleasures, and became their slave. The Greeks were not interested in the question of naturalness or unnaturalness with regard
to the – for them central – eroticism of boys, nor the manner of their
pleasure with them. It was rather a question of moderation as
prerequisite for a virile self-control. It was the quantity, not the
quality of the *aphrodisia* which concerned conceptions of morality
in the ancient world. The 'natural desire only consists in satisfying
needs' (UP 45). The Greek man was concerned not with the truth of
desire, nor how one constitutes oneself as a 'sexual being', nor with
the exaggeration of the sexual, as it is monstrously embodied in the
modern concept of sexuality, but with a restraint, an adjustment of
the free power of sexual pleasures. The essential in this was to
avoid excess and passivity in dealing with pleasures. Pleasure in
itself was not 'bad' or 'reprehensible' for the Greeks, but 'the "stasi-
atic" potential of the sexual appetite' (UP 49) demanded its moral
discrimination. From this arose a complex game of behaviour
modes, focusing around this virtuality of excess, a game whose
object was to devote particular attention to the dangers of an
unmodulated use of pleasures.

For the attitude, the position of the individual in the force and
tension fields of the pleasures, for the free Greek man, therefore,
the model of penetration was decisive. According to this the practice of *aphrodisia* depended on the basic difference of whether one
was object or subject, penetrated or penetrator, active or passive,
commanding or devoted, man or boy/woman. As long as the
sexual act was practiced moderately, it was unproblematic and of
secondary interest. The question was posed, however, regarding
'the one who performs the activity and the one on whom it is
performed' (UP 47).

The penetration model reiterates here that it was a male morality
which governed Greek ethics. For the Greeks, the question of the
sexual essence of the man–woman–relationship, as it is problematized today, was unthinkable due to the clear dividing line
between the sexes which was predetermined by the penetration
model. Sigmund Freud's admission that he did not know what
woman desires, is typical for that part of hermeneutical discourse
or for psychoanalytical attempt at a theory of the subject, which has
no equivalent in Greek thought. For the men of Greek antiquity,
where the position of the woman depended solely on that of
the man, and therefore was also not reflected in terms such as

'oppression', the woman was not the primary object of a moral concern. 'Phallocentrism' (if we can allow this anachronism), as a paraphrasing of man's dominant position towards the woman, was perfectly unproblematic for the Greeks in the framework of their male morality which by definition was made for men. It only takes on a pejorative sense in twentieth century psychoanalysis by the continued attempt to place the supposedly hidden 'woman's desire' in clear relation to that of the man. This kind of theoretical construction of desire is foreign to antiquity. From this we should not conclude that Foucault's studies favoured a certain model of moral experience, in order to develop a critique of present-day conceptions from this viewpoint. He was rather concerned with 'the proximity and the difference to be made visible and thus, by way of their rules, to show how the same advice given by ancient morality can play a different role in the style of contemporary morality' (DE 4/701).

In Greek moral reflection the use of pleasures, the '*chrēsis aphro-disiōn*, depended on strategies of need, timeliness, and status' (UP 54). Along these strategies a technology of self develops which aims at mastering the pleasures. This control is not considered nega-tively as a discrimination of the flesh, as it is later applied by Christian pastoral in a moral codex, but as a natural force – which characterizes the dynamic element of pleasures.

The first strategy, which Foucault introduced later in the second volume of *The History of Sexuality*, is that of need. A particularly decisive function is attached to this in the development of ethical substance. Furthermore, through this strategy a significant differ-ence to the present becomes clear, which Foucault implicitly emphasized: the fundamental opposition to the hermeneutical subject of desire. For the Greeks, it was not desire which dictated the needs and constructed a 'sexual identity' for the man, but the need that roused desire. This reversal gave the key target of psychoanalysis discourse quite a different perspective: In the male world of antiquity, a practical, action-orientated use of pleasures took the place of an apparently endless hermeneutics of desire. The Greek formula of a three-parted sexual behaviour – actions, pleasure and desire – was thus diametrically opposed to the modern one.

ASKESIS AS EXISTENTIAL EXERCISE

It is the body itself, its sexual and nutritional needs, which were placed in subordination to a regulating activity, for only what was needful for the body counted. But in antiquity there were no exact regulations or laws which prescribed where a need's definitive limits lay, or how far it was bound to a natural order. Instead of snatching the secret of desire from the depths of the unconscious where it had been forced by a complex process of sublimation, in antiquity the concern for moderation applied, and hence the control of the pleasures. These revealed their activity far more on the surface than in unconscious depths. The principle of moderation was a form of permanent self-restriction, in as far as it was meant to prevent an excess of pleasures, and to trace back continuously to the reason of the need. The natural need has a regulating effect with regard to the excessive dynamics of the *aphrodisia*. For the Greeks satisfying a need meant satisfying it at the right moment in time (*kairos*), and not having a desire which on the one hand had to be 'liberated' and on the other had to be 'sublimated'. In this strategic game, it was far more a question of maintaining the pleasures than suppressing them. The use of pleasures included the art of distributing them over the course of one's existence, without them becoming an existential obstacle.

The aim of this moderating approach to the *aphrodisia* was a stylization of the self, trying, beyond the *chrēsis aphrodisiōn*, 'to make one's life into a brilliant work' (UP 60). In this sense, virtue derived from the ability to gauge each individual beneficial limit with regard to pleasures in a daily work on oneself. In contrast to the 'legal subject' which bases its actions on a law or a social moral code, the ethics of antiquity existed in the art (*technē*) 'that by taking general principles into account would guide action in its time, according to its context, and in view of its ends. Therefore, in this form of morality, the individual did not make himself into an ethical subject by universalizing the principles that informed his action; on the contrary, he did so by means of an attitude and a quest that individualized his action, modulated it, and perhaps even gave him a special brilliance by virtue of the rational and deliberate structure his action manifested' (UP 62).

The use of pleasures required control of them. *Enkrateia*, as Foucault attempted to define it, was essentially a balance of the individual with himself; it was an attitude of the individual towards himself through self-control. The attitude, the type of self-relation, was for the Greeks an agonistic, competitive, fighting relation, a work on oneself where 'speech, deed, and art' (UP 66) determined the scope of the action. The teleology of *agōn* was self-mastery, the taming of the pleasures, the warlike wrestling for a power which one measured first against oneself, in order to be able to measure it against opponents later. The agonistic understanding of power in antiquity was, however, not primarily directed at the opponent, but was constituted as an ethical principle of self-discipline. An agonistic relation meant engaging in single combat with oneself and discovering the correct limit for one's strengths. It was an 'antagonism of oneself toward oneself' which should 'structure the ethical attitude of the individual vis-à-vis desires and pleasures' (UP 68).

In the pagan ethics of antiquity, a technology of the self was opposed to a Christian denial of the self with regard to obedience to God, and to those confessions of the flesh which served the discrimination of the pleasures. The technology of the self actually presupposed for the management of the self an affirmative relation to desires and to life. Foucault's development of this attitude of self-stylization through a measured use of pleasures not only made clear the essential differences to Christian ethics which were themes in the unpublished fourth volume of *The History of Sexuality*, but also extended the genealogical line up to that subject who 'acquits' himself in the psychoanalytical situation. There is always an immanent criticism of the hermeneutics of desire in Foucault's analysis of pagan ethics. Foucault gave the heautocraty of the ancient subject precedence over the self-deciphering, cathartic subject.

The actions which a Greek had to perform in order to bring about a correct use of his power – or more precisely, to bring out his inner strengths, his energies – were accompanied by one of the Socratic lessons, to which Foucault paid particular attention in his analysis: He introduced the term *askēsis*, which is not to be confused with the Christian understanding of this concept, but which is used and interpreted in its original pagan meaning. Askēsis is an exercise on oneself which neither denies nor stigmatizes the pleasures, but aims at using them correctly, i.e. moderately. Self-control is its fundamental ideal.

While Christian asceticism is connected with a religious doctrine of salvation which proclaims the divine promise of resurrection beyond the transient human life, the pagan askēsis of the Greeks was founded on the care of the self, the *epimeleia heautou*. Of interest to the Greeks was not the ideal of loving thy neighbour, but that of conducting oneself in order to lead others and to be an example to them. Self-concern was the prerequisite from which relations to others were to be shaped. Askēsis was seen by the Greeks as an exercise which served 'to reduce every pleasure to nothing more than the elementary satisfaction of needs. Considered as a whole, this exercise implied a reduction to nature, a victory over self, and a natural economy that would produce a life of real satisfactions' (UP 73).

Foucault stressed that this askēsis by means of practice – or more precisely: through many continual practices – was not specified or subject to a generally binding code which would call the free man to obligatory practices. Rather the exercise should secure a certain behaviour through the rigour with which it was regarded. The path of ascetic practice was supposed to enable self-government, in order to allow government of others. This was on the condition that the power practised on oneself and others was measured by the same rule, and that the severity towards others was in a reciprocal relation to the rigour towards oneself. The 'master of himself and the master of others received the same training' (UP 77). Through this basic self-restriction of power practice, one conformed to the ethical principle of moderation which helped prevent a hubristic use or misuse of power. Askēsis thus was the ethical-moral armour of the free man, guaranteeing the circumspect use of his power, and consequently his freedom. Freedom was not a given value at the disposal of everyone, but signified sovereignty, which was first to be gained through unceasing work on oneself, in order finally to become master of one's pleasures and not their slave. To be slave and therefore dominated was the opposition to the free sovereign man. Only in the sovereign use of power over oneself did one attain the freedom of political leadership within the city. The highest virtue of moderation was represented by the one who, through self-mastery, was also able to lead others without becoming immoderate.

The fact that moderation in the male morality of antiquity was a virile virtue, effective with regard to male pleasures, had its basis in the fundamental isomorphism inherent to this morality. 'Self-mastery was a way of being a man with respect to oneself' (UP 82) and thus to be able to take on an exemplary function for other men. Against this background, Foucault explained why the most important object of concern in the Greek moral reflection was the boy, not the woman. For the boy was the one onto whom that virile virtue was transferable within a monosexually orientated male-dominated society.

The male morality of the Greeks did not pass judgement on different types of sexual behaviour; it did not, then, differentiate the morphology of the pleasures. The deciding moral criterium, however, was the style of activity, whether someone was active or passive, male or female, moderate or excessive. This attitude is not comparable to the present-day differentiation between heterosexual and homosexual actions, or even identities. For the Greeks, the 'ethical negativity' (UP 85) did not lie in the choice of the object itself, nor whether a boy or a woman was the object of desire, but – and here is a crucial point of pagan askēsis which is particularly emphasized by Foucault – whether one behaved passively in relation to one's pleasures.

SELF-ASSAY AND THE STYLISTICS OF LIFE

The attitude of the Greek man, for whom moderation and self-control in his dealings with pleasures formed ethical constituents of a genuine virility, was at the same time a type of self-knowing. The ancient form of self-constitution was still 'unburdened' by an identity-forming 'truth' of desire, as is still characteristic of our century. In antiquity, the knowledge of 'sexuality' had not yet been rearranged by a scientific discourse which tried to label people with the truth about themselves. Science was a quite different thing from that which is understood by the term today. It was a form of knowledge bound up with moderation itself, in as far as one 'could not form oneself as an ethical subject in the use of pleasures without forming oneself at the same time as a subject of knowledge' (UP 86).

Access to self-knowledge conveyed itself not simply through a comprehensive knowledge *of* desires, but through the practice of self-constitution which made dealings *with* the desires into a moral problem. For Foucault it seemed of particular interest here that the use of reason (*logos*) served above all for a problematization of the present situation, in which a man attempted to measure and constitute himself in relation to his actions. In this, for Foucault, the ancient culture of the self was in opposition to the 'modern cult of the self', whose concept is based on a self which merely has to be found in order to emancipate oneself from supposed constraints and to 'discover' one's 'authentic' self.[12]

Reason itself served in the never-ending task and art of finding the correct centre of one's life, of guaranteeing the status of the free, active man through a moderating practice of all pleasures. For such an ethics of moderation, in which freedom was considered as nothing other than a forming of the self, it was not an outwardly directed hope of 'another life', or a 'true' self from which existential questions could be answered which was crucial, but, on the contrary, the relation which one had to oneself. It was not the task of the *logos* to find universal rules for a correct conduct valid for the whole, but to strive for individual maturity through a fundamental self-relation of ethical work. Foucault termed this 'ontological recognition of the self by the self' (UP 88).

In the light of these later writings and Foucault's – for many surprising – thematization of classical culture of the self, the intention of such books as *The Order of Things*, which established him as the great Nietzschean genealogist, becomes clear: The death of man as proclaimed by Foucault in the example of humanism is not based so much on nihilism. Rather, all his life Foucault pursued a 'demasking of the subject' through a genealogical analysis of the circumstances and factors which constituted the subject into what he appears in the present. Beyond these limits is neither the transcendental subject of Kant, nor Sartre's existential subject, but the ethical effort of the individual to give his life a beautiful form.

In the knowledge of oneself, reason achieves that rigour and severity required for the control of the desires. The inner order (*kosmos*) of the self, the equilibristic relation of body and mind, is the limit and basis for the truth about oneself which can be attained in the form of self-knowledge. In this manner, ethical guidelines find vivid expression in the individual himself, whose relation to truth is not constituted by regulations or any ethical considerations beyond personal experience. 'The relation to truth was a structural, instrumental, and ontological condition for establishing the individual as a moderate subject leading a life of moderation; it was not an epistemological condition enabling the individual to recognize himself in his singularity as a desiring subject and to purify himself of the desire that was thus brought to light' (UP 89).

Control of the desires was not the sole point of attention in ancient Greek morality. The telos of the individual, whose access to truth required knowledge of the self, was given precedence over a mere use of the pleasures. But what was the 'sense' of ethics which asserted no universal rights, and of which the epistemological prerequisite was characterized by a *logos* supposed to structure (virile) freedom on the level of moderation?

Foucault's ethical problematizations here and elsewhere – as will be shown later – are deeply rooted in Nietzsche's thought. Should the philosophical tug-of-war for the truth be decided in favour of a hermeneutics of desire and an ontology of lack, or in favour of a fundamental contingency of existence, which is to be '*justified* only as an aesthetic phenomenon'? (1/17,47; 3/464) For Foucault, the aesthetical premise in early Nietzsche is vital for an aesthetics of existence problematized in ancient Greece as a 'moderate existence whose hallmark, grounded in truth, was both its regard for an ontological structure and its visibly beautiful shape' (UP 89). Truth is not eternal or universal, it is based on no metaphysical assumption, nor does it tempt with some shining distant ideal; truth remains a chimera as long as it is considered merely as something released from the inner order. For only from this self-constituted order, from the will for stylization, can the individual make of his life a beautiful work. In the place of meaning or of a religious promise which sees the question of sense in a life beyond earthly pleasures and physiological facts, steps the brilliance of an individual lifestyle, in which the individual knows how to style himself into an object of joy for himself and for others in *this* world. From this supposed meaning of life there develops a beautiful existence, a 'self-enchantment' which cannot be defamed as narcissism, but which is the result of an ethical work on oneself.

Since the anarchic forces at work in them required their control, the *aphrodisia* formed an important component of ancient Greek moral reflection. Assuming the *aphrodisia* as ethical substance, Foucault attempted to show which ascetic technologies were employed in order to become master of oneself. Instead of an adherence to laws or codifications of behaviour, later to peak in a hermeneutics of the subject propelled by psychoanalysis, Foucault described the 'stylization of attitude' and an aesthetics of existence which in antiquity obeyed a necessity inherent to life itself, and which took into account an ethical masculinity. Each individually composed life should take on the form of a moderated existence in which one's own needs were satisfied in a manner in keeping with nature, without exceeding beneficial limits.

DIETETICS

For the Greeks, the regimen of the body was a broad field of moral problematization, since it formed the area of tension between the need and its appropriate, but not immoderate, satisfaction. For this reason, medicine in antiquity was of a dietetic rather than a thera-peutic kind, in which a correct diet formed the basis for the health and resistance of the body. According to Foucault's estimation, concern regarding the correct diet was far greater than concern regarding sexual pleasures. For the Greeks, the protection of the body from potential diseases by way of a prophylactic in the sense of appropriate dietetics was a concern fundamentally characteriz-ing daily life. In contrast to modern medicine, which is primarily given a negative definition of a pathology by diagnosis and treat-ment, the dietetic lifestyle of the Greeks was a 'medical science' in which care of the body depended on its individual beneficial limit. Physiology was far more important than pathology.

Greek dietetics was no cult which glorified and fetishized the body. Nor was the body an object of a militaristic toughening up programme aiming at its institutional assimilation. The goal was to establish a harmony between body and soul for the benefit of a comprehensive aesthetics of existence. The body, similarly to the *aphrodisia*, was also an ethical substance in so far as its fashioning contributed to an aesthetics of existence. In Greek dietetics, both the athlete, tending to overproportion and all too zealous in tough-ening himself,[13] and the hypochondriac, harming himself with exaggerated adherence to nutritional rules, and who in the end only teetered on the brink of death, were discredited as examples of excess.

Along with this practice of moderation, which tried to avoid both excess and understatement, dietetics contained a strategic aspect which problematized the flexibility of a possible dietetic order. Instead of a rigid 'diet plan' upon which the individual was supposed to base the regulation of his physical regimen, it was more important to adapt dietetics to the circumstances, which required different measures according to age, place and time. Furthermore, the correct limit depended on each individual's economic needs and was not necessarily valid for everyone. For a particular diet, good for one person, might not be so for another. The flexibility of dietetics was more important than its one-sided dogmatization. The care of the self as a care for the dietetic precautionary measures with regards to the body was a reflecting activity, through which awareness of one's physical condition and requirements was heightened. In this way, dietetics assumed an indispensable role within a moral reflection serving self-constitution: control of the body was prerequisite for the control of oneself.

Foucault also clearly emphasized the ancient principle of moderation with regard to the dietetics of sexual acts. The sexual act as such was not of interest to the Greeks. The quality or truth of the desire was not inquired after, but the quantity of *aphrodisia* was problematized. The actual concern for the Greeks was to make the *aphrodisia* serve one's own enjoyment without taking harm by exceeding the limit. For this, a restrictive economy was needed, in order to master those forces tending to hubris which are inherent in the pleasures. The Greeks measured a restrictive economy of male sexuality by the ejaculation model, in which profligacy and abstinence could be symbolized. In order to practise control over oneself, the seductive force of the *aphrodisia* had to be resisted; one should not allow oneself to be 'overmastered' by this force.

By portraying these moral problematizations, central to antiquity, Foucault was trying to show that the Greeks did not simply have a permissive sexual life. Far from an age of the 'sexual revolution' and the belief that sexuality has merely to be freed from repression, it was precisely a moderated attitude towards the *aphrodisia* which, for the Greeks, was indispensable for the maintenance of their liberty, in that sexual excess was accompanied by an enslaving of the self. 'The sexual act did not occasion anxiety because it was associated with evil but because it disturbed and threatened the individual's relationship with himself and his integrity as an ethical subject in the making; if it was not properly measured and distributed' (UP 136), it could lead to an existential crisis.

The juridical model of an unreflected loyalty to the law was opposed in the ancient world by a technique of living which should lead to the constitution of oneself and the ethical formation of the subject. This management of oneself, giving one's life a form of beauty and creating from it a work, essentially differentiated the Greek man concerned with self-control from the later godfearing Christian subject to a 'herd morality'. The free man modelled himself as an artwork of himself, not by discriminating against his forces, but by masculine conduct towards them. A pagan self-forming preceded later Christianity's divine doctrine of salvation.

ASYMMETRICAL RELATIONSHIPS

Man and Woman

The ancient Greek moral reflection, based on a virile self-relation, precluded a symmetrical bond between man and woman, being concerned instead with a responsibility towards the boy as future free man. Marriage in antiquity was determined neither by an affective nor an idealistic relationship, but by the natural bond of an economy whose counterpart was essentially in a reflection on the house (*oikos*). The use of pleasures was not a moral problem in the relationship to the wife, but was founded on the demand for virile self-control described above. Thus, reflection on the use of *aphrodisia* was directed less towards the wife than towards the relationship which the man maintained towards himself or the boy.

The bond of marriage in ancient Greece differed therefore in essential points from the Christian marriage, which even today is particularly protected as a social institution by national constitutions, and which, as the state's basic social structure, receives authorization. This monopoly of marriage did not exist in the male-dominated society of ancient Greece, for which it would be rather a paradox. The social position of the free man within the city was dependent not on his role as husband, but on his ability to govern himself and others – including his wife and the household under her care. A central role was attached to his 'governmentality', as the stylization of his power.

Governmentality as '"economic" art' (UP 153) took on much sharper contours in the administration of one's own property and house than would be visible in a more abstract fashion in the example of the city. The government qualities necessary for the *oikos* and the guiding of the woman, were, for the Greeks, part of a comprehensive pedagogical strategy which was not fixed institutionally. Beyond the agonistically structured relationships between free men, there existed a pedagogy which reflected its own order with regard to the household and marriage. This order applied to the *oikos* was defined by the fundamental asymmetrical relationship between man and woman. The community between the two spouses was primarily based on concern for the household, and within which order the roles complemented each other. While the woman took care of the interior of the house, and maintained her rule within the domestic order, the man was responsible for the external sphere. In this fashion, the community of man and woman was not linked by the higher ideal of love, but by the recognition of the need to master life together. In his analysis of the ancient Greek marriage relationship, Foucault distinguished three value categories, very sober-sounding to modern ears, which essentially constituted the bond of marriage: community of property, community of living and community of body.

Apart from this 'external order' there also existed an 'internal' one between the spouses: Self-control (*enkrateia*). This should prevent the sexual attraction of the spouses from exceeding the natural limit. Although subjected to the man's rule, the woman should not, as mere object, serve the man's desire and the increase of his pleasure. Her prime position depended on the management of the household, not seduction of the husband. Not the art of make-up for pleasing the man was considered virtuous, but the woman's ability to style herself through her allotted occupations as mistress of the house. The upright posture and carriage gave her body that attitude and form, which, for the Greeks, 'characterized the physique of the free individual' (UP 162). Within her own sphere, the *oikos*, the woman achieved her own sovereignty in spite of the man's rule. 'In this way the body's handsomeness will be shaped and maintained; the condition of mastery has its physical version, which is beauty' (UP 162–3).

Foucault is not analysing here any so-called 'misogyny' of ancient Greek male-dominated society, which later brought him the criticism already mentioned. Rather it was the attempt to show that the woman, although subjugated to the virile virtues, was capable of styling her own beauty within her sphere of command. In this Foucault was trying to convey a conception of beauty which appeared to be fundamental to ancient aesthetics of existence: Beauty, not in a conventional 'cosmetic' sense, but as a beauty of the 'inner cosmos' for which, in the woman's case, her work and sovereignty as mistress of the house was decisive. It was the command she had over domestic concerns, a command which accorded her a privileged position. Her physical beauty and her attitude as mistress of the house were constituted from proficient use of this command. Foucault did not wish to diagnose woman's sufficiently well-known dependence on man in the male-dominated society of ancient Greece, but to show that sovereignty and conduct have their plastic physical expression in the individual – regardless of gender.

Foucault's portrayal of ancient attitude is by no means some absurd plea for woman's domestic role, nor otherwise influenced by any misogynous intentions. He wished to show that the interplay between power and beauty has not lost its relevance for women in so-called modern society. A person's physiognomy can serve here as an illuminating example of Foucault's non gender-specific statement that the position of power has its physical side, that is beauty. Beyond a traditionally allocated role and the dominating ideal of a natural, even 'god-given' bond between the sexes, the woman also has the opportunity to cultivate her own sovereignty and beauty. What might obstruct this sovereignty today are those identities, prescribed by social morality, and so often rejected by Foucault, which are assumed and reproduced by both men and women. A feminist critique, which considers the situation of the woman from the position of the victim-role, and thus calls to account the 'patriarchal heritage', itself moves within an all too gender-specific identity allocation. Here lies an important reason for Foucault's emphasis on a 'monosexual culture' – to be commented on later – which, for both sexes, on the basis of their respective natural orders, could be the opportunity for another culture and new thought and behaviour patterns released from the shackles of tradition.

The fundamental problem which Foucault was trying to highlight through the example of Xenophon's text *Oeconomicus* was less an economy of marriage than an economy of government which – in a virile morality – was necessarily linked to the techniques of self-control. For command over others was simultaneously connected to command over oneself. The *oikos* could not be administered, the servants not given orders if one had not exercised a moderate use of one's own power, and was no slave of pleasure. Within this ethical order – which, it should be noted, did not aim at any ethical theory, nor precondition for any such theory in antiquity – the concept of politics between individual and city also finds its practical meaning as the art of governing oneself. Constituting oneself as moral subject was essentially a question of mastery over oneself. In this respect, Foucault did not view the ancient city (*polis*), according to his analysis, as an organization form comparable to the modern state system. In the place of loyalty to the state and its laws, the free man was faced with the problem of governing himself. It was not obedience to the laws of the city which was the main ethical and moral concern of the Greeks, but rather the self-fashioning of the free man which was prerequisite for a city capable of government. The self-concern characteristic of ancient Greece laid the foundation for leading a 'political' life, and consequently, for leading others. For the man – whether in the city or his own house – governing himself was the basic ethical concern upon which his behaviour to others depended. This form of particular political relationship also interested Foucault in his final lectures on 'governmentality', which will be referred to elsewhere.

Foucault always linked the form of power practice on oneself and others with a central aspect of ancient moral reflection: moderation. Moderation did not revolve around the wife, but around the man's will 'to give his life a certain form. A matter of style, as it were: the man is called upon to temper his conduct in terms of the mastery he intends to bring to bear on himself, and in terms of the moderation with which he aims to exercise his mastery over others' (UP 182). For the husband, the integrity of his existence was unrelated to the legally settled relations with his wife. For Foucault, this also explained the fact that apart from the concern for their mutual offspring and the administration of the house, the marriage relationship itself, in contrast to moderation, was scarcely ever problematized. There was a clear demarcation line between the sexes. The relationship to oneself was far more significant than a marriage founded on the ideal of partnership. Whilst the woman's self-relation was gauged against the model of the man's mastery over himself, her relationship to the man was characterized by the format of obedience and compliance to his will. For the man, mastery over himself had prominence over management of his household and his wife. Concern for a moderated exercise of power was the crux of 'an ethics of self-delimiting domination' (UP 184).

Man and Boy

Belonging to the most problematic area of Greek moral reflection was love of boys. This love was not, as often suggested by present-day portrayals of this aspect of ancient history, the result of any particular permissiveness or greater tolerance of homosexuality in the ancient world. As described at the start, any such concept of sexuality – let alone a concept of homosexuality – as prevails in modern society, did not even exist for the Greeks. It was not the kind of desire, nor the question as to its object, but self-control and moderation which counted among the more important problem areas of ancient moral reflection. For the free man, there was nothing reprehensible in love of boys. This love only became a problem if the man became excessive in his behaviour and thus a slave to his pleasures – contrary to his status of free citizen which required him to be an example to the boy of a moderate way of life.

It was no social phenomenon that Foucault was studying in this love of boys, neither did he ask about the specificity of a desire. 'We need to take up the question afresh, using terms other than those of "tolerance" toward "homosexuality"' (UP 191). Foucault had already explained in the first volume of *The History of Sexuality* why the use of expressions like 'repression' and 'emancipation' appeared inadequate to him. He also categorically rejected a psychoanalytical understanding of the 'polymorphous pervert'. Instead of presenting the hermeneutics of ancient Greek sexual behaviour, he attempted to revive the complex 'interplay of positive and negative appraisals' (UP 191) which accompanied same-sex love in ancient moral reflection. For Foucault, it was not significant whether or not the Greeks were 'pederasts' or 'homosexuals', but that the love of boys 'gave rise to a whole cultural elaboration' (UP 214). This cultural elaboration, as it was expressed in the ethical problematization of antiquity, was the subject of Foucault's final studies.

In antiquity the relationship to the wife was scarcely ever problematized, because its form was already predetermined by its legal nature, and the free man's power was clearly delineated by the woman's duty of obedience. A man's relationship to the boy, on the other hand, was defined by a crucial contradiction which necessitated an appropriate stylistics in the use of the pleasures. Furthermore, reflection on same-sex love did not presuppose a relationship between two grown men of the same age, as would be consistent with the general conception of homosexuality today. The outer core of the problematic was formed by an asymmetry between the boy as beloved (*eromenos*) and his much older lover (*erastes*) on the one hand, and the polarity, so typical of the Greeks, of active and passive sexual behaviour on the other. The inner core was concern for the boy himself, whose 'denigration' into a passive object of pleasure was unacceptable, since the boy was to be prepared for his future role as free man. The boy's submissive attitude in his passive role was in stark contrast to his future active position as free citizen. This asymmetry, therefore, fundamentally influenced the love of boys, and was also the premise for Plato's attempt to give love of wisdom precedence over the asymmetrical relationship of such love, thus setting the course towards a concern which distracted from the boy.

For Foucault, however, the problem of the love of boys was not simply reduced to a pedagogical strategy; such a view would correspond to the traditional image of a pedagogic model, according to which the 'pederastic' preference of the Greeks was linked exclusively to an educational duty of care. Instead, Foucault drew attention to the behaviour rituals which extended beyond such a duty. 'Even before they were taken up by philosophical reflection, these relations were already the pretext for a whole social game' (UP 196). Thus Foucault, referring to the – for him – influential works of Kenneth J. Dover and John Boswell, corrected the history of a prejudice which continues right into today's academic circles as an urge to justify opposition to same-sex lifestyles. From a historiography which had allowed the love of boys and its fundamental social significance in Greek antiquity to fall into oblivion, Foucault guided the reader back towards a lively game of courtship between *erastes* and *eromenos*, lover and beloved. At the same time he made it clear that their relationship was not something which was taken for granted, precisely because, in comparison to the starkly rigid legal status of marriage, it was an open game.

A characteristic locus in Greek male-dominated society was the *gymnasium*. It was not simply the institutionalized form of ancient pedagogy and was by no means comparable to our contemporary school system, geared towards the needs of the modern state. Rather, it was first and foremost a meeting place, where boys were courted. It was the setting for a social game in which the older *erastes* had no 'statutory authority' (UP 198) over the boy. For in contrast to slaves, the boy could not, as future free man, be at anyone's disposal, nor given orders. For the older lover, the rule applied above all, to respect the boy's freedom and not force him into anything. The boy's love had to be fought for, he had to be 'chased' and rivals for his favour had to be outdone.

The boy's special worth lay in his beauty and youth, which made his body desirable for a limited time. With the onset of beard growth and other physical signs of adulthood the bloom faded. This aesthetic and erotic appreciation of the boy's physique was accompanied by a morality which gave expression to the ambivalence of this intrinsically limited beauty. By nature, the boy lacked a masculine appearance, but virile morals did not permit him to be soft or feminine. The boy was urged to prepare himself with physical exercises for his role as potentially free man. The magic which the boy exerted on the *erastes* originated less from his androgynous appearance than from his inherent nature, which was highly influenced by approaching masculinity, and, for this very reason, required the care of the older lover, endowed with the virile attributes. The boy as future free man was not only the object of sexual desire, but his body, already carrying the essential features of the later man, was also the object of a concern arising from the awareness of his future role.

Ancient concern for the boy found specific moral form in a reflection on Eros and its essence. The fact that this reflection was not directed at the marriage model was not because the 'homosexual desire' was felt by the Greeks to be a problematic contradiction to reproductive heterosexuality.[14] Foucault referred to another difference, standing in opposition to the legal nature of marriage: Precisely because the relationship of lover and beloved was not fixed institutionally and instead was accompanied by a ritual, playful art of love, the relationship itself was the point from which its form was problematized.

Here too, the primary basis for a moral reflection forming around eroticism of boys was concern for oneself and the constituting of oneself as moral subject. For, as future free man, the boy was the potential subject of virile virtues like moderation and self-control. In this sense, the older lover found the self-relation of the free individual reflected in the boy: in the responsibility towards himself on the one hand, and in the instruction of the boy in attainment of virile virtues on the other. This special relationship between *erastes* and his *eromenos* can also be seen as an 'ethical isomorphism', a fundamental congruence, in that both boy and man belonged to the same male morality. For the erotics which formed around the boy aimed beyond the problematic of the *aphrodisia*, and applied to the boy not only in that he was the older man's love object, but precisely in that he was also the focus of ethical behaviour.

The boy's honour is a further example by which Foucault

demonstrated the absurdity of a concept of sexual permissiveness among the Greeks. To prevent him from being degraded to the level of a freely disposable object of pleasure for the *erastes*, and to protect him from the humiliation of being helplessly delivered up to the older lover's attentions, it was considered dishonourable to approach the boy in any other way than from a distance and by playful courting. For the boy's honour made a crucial contribution to his preparation for his future role in the city, and to the development of his qualities as free citizen. In his own interest, the boy had to ensure that his conduct conformed to the basic characteristics of virile morals; that he was moderate and endowed his life with an early maturity honourable to him, qualifying him so much better as future master over himself and others. It was 'a time when his worth was tested, in the sense that it had to be formed, exercised, and measured all at the same time' (UP 206). The importance of the adolescent time lay in its testing nature, in the manner in which the boy proved himself with regards to a consolidating constitution of himself as moral subject. In this the agonistic relation to himself and others – including his relationship to the *erastes* – was to be exercised as a game of conflict which enabled the free man to measure his strengths.

The ethos of the boy was visible to others through his behaviour. It was expressed in situations of everyday life, and in dealings with other boys and men: 'by his dress, by his bearing, by his gait, by the poise with which he reacts to events, etc.' (DE 4/714). The boy's self-control could be gauged by, and assume form through, his way of life. The boy in ancient Greece was prepared for his future role as citizen, less through so-called all-round education than through an agonistic attitude which he adopted towards both himself and his older lover, who acted as model: A far cry from modern educational establishments and the public servants academically prepared especially for them.[15] The Greeks would have considered a 'humanistic education ideal', based on a high regard for wide knowledge and on the dominance of intellectual values, as excessive and a hindrance to the constitution of oneself as moral subject. Instead of an accumulation of knowledge which is prerequisite today for further qualifications and the preparation of 'professionals', knowledge was also subject to the law of moderation and the prime ethical demand for self-formation. It is for this reason above all that command of the pleasures, and not intellectual predominance, was the expression of and premise for a self-relation which predetermined, so to speak, the relationship to valuable knowledge.

If we may allow another anachronism to highlight the funda-mental difference between the ancient and modern worlds – the present-day model of coeducation would have represented for the Greeks an obstacle to the pedagogical aim of training the boy through a constant attentiveness towards himself. Concern for the boy related to his attitude towards his maturing virile virtues, and to an ethical masculinity dependent on them.

It was not only through self-relation that Foucault explained the vital role of moderation in ancient moral reflection. It was also an indispensable indicator in the erotic game between *eromenos* and *erastes*. The boy was expected to display moderation as a sign of a virtuous reserve, and in this way could raise his worth as an object of love. Boys who easily succumbed to their lover's courtship, or even – in the most comprehensive sense of this word – prostituted themselves, were considered soft, and had a bad reputation; deal-ings with them or with those lovers who courted them, was taboo.

What Foucault analysed as the ethics of the free man concerning a correct use of the pleasures (*orthōs chrēsthai*) – also applicable to the boy – was mirrored in the comprehensive concern for oneself (*epimeleia heautou*). This Socratic principle of self-care by which knowledge was essentially seen as 'self-knowledge', constituted itself by means of a permanent problematization and exercise with regard to one's own lifestyle. Characterizing both *eromenos* and *erastes* was an endless contest (*agōn*), a daily wrestling with one's own forces, prevailing over them and ultimately being able to give them a form within the stylization of one's own life. The purpose of such a self-testing philosophy was to help in being 'stronger than oneself' (UP 211).

Both the boy's body, as a yet unfinished work and an expression of his own unique beauty, and his life (*bios*) as a whole, necessitated a strict testing and styling of himself. Yet besides general concern for the boy's education, pleasure in him was the actual problematic aspect with regard to the moral reflection upon the fundamentally asymmetrical relationship between unequal lovers. Here too, Foucault assumed that moral reflection on the *aphrodisia* was based on 'the principle of isomorphism between sexual relations and social relations' (UP 215). In order to enact his role in the house or in the city according to his masculine position, the free man must always be the active, dominant one. Within a morality conceived for and by men, the penetration model was therefore paramount in determining what should be classified as ethically negative or reprehensible. No such isomorphism, however, was given for the position of the boy, who was not yet in possession of the free man's rights as citizen and was obliged to practice filial obedience: The isomorphism prerequisite for the free man was merely anticipated.

The reflection upon the boy as the free man's object of pleasure fell within the tension area of, on the one hand, the privileges already enjoyed by the boy through his role as future citizen, and on the other, his yet unattained maturity and his consequent need for guidance. In his studies of the classical texts, Foucault ascertained a noticeable silence regarding the Greek's sexual pleasures in the boy. For it was evident that the boy as object of pleasure was dominated by the penetrating older lover. In this subjugated role, the boy hardly conformed to the ethos of male superiority' (UP 220) which carried such pedagogical weight. This 'antinomy of the boy' (UP 221) was insoluble; between the claim of ethics and pederastic practice there existed in moral reflection an unbridgeable discrepancy which was at most alleviated by the attempt to set limits to the boy's status as pleasure object. One such limitation was the 'coldness' of the boy who succumbed to the pleasure and desire of the *erastes*. The boy was not permitted to find enjoyment in the role of the one penetrated. 'Between the man and the boy, there is not – there cannot and should not be – a community of pleasure' (UP 223). Instead of feeling pleasure in the penetration act, the boy should see his submission solely as a favour granted to the *erastes*.

The asymmetry in the relationship to the boys, problematic for the Greeks, and the difficulty posed by its moral integration, was seen by Foucault as paving the way for a relationship in which the boy was not degraded to the level of pleasure object: The new relationship should have the form of friendship (*philia*). In Foucault's view, the decisive turning point of a comprehensive pederastic practice, pausing before the great Socratic reflection on Eros, now began to emerge, giving the ancient love of boys an essentially new quality: 'how to make the object of pleasure into a subject who was in control of his pleasures' (UP 225).

SEXUALITY AND TRUTH

For the Greeks, the 'problem of considering the boy as an object of pleasure' (UP 223) was insoluble, and from this problematic there arose a shift of emphasis which Foucault saw manifested in the philosophical eroticism of Socrates – or more precisely – Plato. Thus concern for the truth, as the great theme of Western philosophy, derives from the moral conflict inherent in the love of boys. By describing the history of the problematic relationship between the boy and his older lover in its difficult form, Foucault thus prepared for Plato's discourse on the essence of love, and clarified the background to Platonic erotics. Unlike Freud in *his* later writings, Foucault did not deepen or pursue a hermeneutics of desire which was already gradually developing in Plato; instead he expressly recurred to an as yet unidealized 'prehistory' of erotics, which still had its living, tangible form in the lovers' relationship to each other. For his analysis of the transformation of moral reflection revealed in Plato from a problematic, in itself contradictory love of boys, to an erotic ideal in which this contradiction was to be removed, Foucault selected the *Symposium* and *Phaedrus* as his central texts.

With Plato's erotics, the stability of friendship was opposed to the instability and transience of sexual pleasure. Replacing the asymmetry of the love of boys was the symmetry of friendship, no longer problematizing the object's awkward status, but offering, beyond the *aphrodisia*, the prospect of a mutual journey through life, planned and pursued together in equality. The focal point of the new Socratic teaching was not, however, the bond of friendship itself. Forming the core of the philosophical reflection was not the question of conduct within a community between two men and their love for each other; rather it was an 'ontological inquiry' (UP 236) – a question regarding the essence of love itself.

The shift in emphasis first became apparent as a distance towards the boy and his high erotic value. For the boy's beauty dazzled his admirers, who were in danger of 'falling for him' completely and losing sight of themselves. 'So it is necessary to leave off thinking about the beloved and redirect one's inquiry to the one who loves (*to erōn*), questioning him in his own condition' (UP 237). Replacing both the boy as object of love and his power of seduction, was the question as to the 'true' object of love: 'pederasty', as it was characterized in the love behaviour of the *erastes*, became love of truth – philosophy.

At this point it becomes clear once again that for Foucault, the derivation of philosophy in its particular problematization as 'love of truth' was linked to Platonic questioning about the essence of love. The 'love for the truth' arose from the 'antimony of the boy' –

the neuralgic point from which Plato transformed virile moral reflection. This definitive nature of Foucault's interpretation also becomes clear in the German alteration on the title of his last work: Instead of *The History of Sexuality*, the German edition has the less misleading title *Sexuality and Truth*, indicating the specific problematization in Platonic philosophy.

In Foucault's opinion, however, Plato's erotics had not yet established a hermeneutics of desire to which subsequent early Christian morality had simply to attach itself, from thence proceeding on its own transformation into a degradation of the flesh. Plato's interpretation was actually an indicator for the hermeneutic subject of desire which was only later constituted. Plato too, did not yet question the beauty of the body and its erotic appreciation, but the 'truthful love' which it brought into play should henceforth bear a relation to the truth 'beyond the appearances of the object' (UP 239).

In the changing moral reflection of antiquity, love of truth was still linked to the possible relationship between *eromenos* and *erastes*; for the new search and philosophical function, which was now to form the basis of the lovers' relationship, applied to the essence of truth. The distinction love/be loved or passive/active was no longer relevant and the new, reascending ideal of love should bring the lovers together in equality by turning to the truth.

With Plato's demand for the truth of love, the master is recast in the love object's role, and the rights of the boy and his honour are increasingly disputed. Now the master, as the knowledgeable one in command of his pleasures, was to show the beloved the way. The 'mastery that he exercises over himself' (UP 241) authorizes him to demand from others abstinence, continence and moderation towards the *aphrodisia*. Resisting the seductive beauty of the youth distinguished the master above all else: The stronger his art of privation and self-control were, the more passionately was he loved by those still needing knowledge of such an art of restraint.

Representing this new dominant position of the master, who transposed the boy's fragile honour into the ascetic commandment of renunciation, was Socrates. He was the incarnation of that turning point in ancient moral reflection which lent an ascetic attitude to the energy game of the *aphrodisia*; their power, tending to hubris, exposed the free man to the constant danger of becoming slave, and not master, of his desires. Socrates' knowledge of the anarchic forces of the Eros compelled him to a permanent testing of himself in which he attempted to make those forces submissive to him. In this act of self-mastery, truth was the protective shield which enabled him to emerge as cool victor over his passions. The strength with which the Socratic instinct stood up to the *aphrodisia* allowed truth to show through as the result of a duel: Truth was the victor in a game from which one finally emerged stronger than oneself. The relationship to truth was therefore structured by the sovereignty which it was essential to obtain with respect to the *aphrodisia* and in relation to others. The key to one's own sovereignty was the master's wisdom. It was not the boy's honour, but rather the possession of wisdom which determined the new relationship to the object of desire.

This was the beginning of an ethical work already visible in the figure of Socrates, and which was later to be transformed into a hermeneutical one. Out of an erotics of courting the boy's favour there gradually developed an erotics in which Socrates' ascetic ideal had precedence. In this, concern for the boy became concern for the truth and the access to it, both for the *erastes* and the *eromenos*. Following on from an ethics of the pleasures and their correct use was the ascetic attitude of the master who had raised the search for truth to a level of ethical work unknown until that point.

For Foucault, this development by no means disqualified love of boys, nor was it a 'sexual ethics' which excluded the same. Socratic ascetics was rather the affirmative expression for styling and thus enhancing the love of boys, by shaping and forming it. Foucault therefore saw at most only indicators and no sufficient reasons for an early Christian 'revaluation' of pagan moral reflection.

Greek antiquity was not an historical period of 'sexual permissiveness or revolution', but was characterized rather by an ethics of the pleasures and a restrictive economy inherent in this ethics, which should enable a sovereign use of one's pleasures. Fashioned on the basis of this existential concern was, for the Greeks, a form of freedom whose standard lay in the greatest possible independence from desires.

There was no universal law prescribing the possibilities and the limits of such ethics for the art of obtaining control over oneself and styling one's life. The telos of these pagan ethics traced by Foucault was diametrically opposed to the later Christian telos of eternal life in the hereafter: As free man, the Greek was called upon to give form to his conduct, and to create, from the material of his own life, a beautiful, accomplished work. The persistent work on himself and on the design of his life, the relationship attained with himself, enabled him 'to fashion himself into a subject of ethical conduct' (UP 251).

The areas analysed by Foucault of a dietetic, economic and erotic technique of life showed the manner in which the Greeks attempted to lead a restrained, moderate life. Rather than being concerned for 'the salvation of the soul', the ancient Greeks considered it important to give their present life a beautiful and perfect form; a life which retained its lustre for posterity, the proud achievement of one who knew how to master himself and others.

Moderate dealings with the *aphrodisia* needed no legal determination; their problematization was pursued rather as an open game whose rules developed from each individual situation. The Greeks 'felt free to select, adapt, develop and – above all – innovate' (UP 252). In fourth century ancient Greece, the constitution of the sovereign moral subject in self-relation was based on an ethics of moderated power practice and a tempered existence; on an art of existence (*technē tou biou*), whose physical foundation was the body itself, the starting point, in the form of comprehensive dietetics, for the practice of moderation. Attending first to the limits of individual physique, and then gearing one's *logos* of a correct way of life around them, the Greeks developed the art of giving one's whole life a form and allowing it to shine in its perfection. Leading a truthful life did not mean striving for another life which promised truth, but shaping one's relationship to oneself into an access to a comprehensive game of truth. The art was not in the 'depth' of a hermeneutic search for truth, nor in a Christian 'inwardness'; the art arose from the surface of the body itself, the modelling of which was the starting point for a complete work. The Delphic oracle 'know thyself' was, for pagan ethics, the call to the free man to create himself through the process of an 'ethical work'. To be his own demiurge, to give form to the self, which is in itself artificial, was the maxim of the oracle, and of an aesthetics of existence for which the only hereafter lay in creating from one's own existence a work of joy for future generations.

2
A Culture of the Self

DREAM CRITICISM AS A TECHNIQUE OF LIFE

Foucault concluded the second volume of *The History of Sexuality* with the much adopted Platonic–Socratic *Symposium* on the essence of love; he was attempting to make clear that – even if ancient erotics was beginning to be transferred from attention towards the boy to an ascetic attitude of the subject – the turning point personified by Socrates did not yet approach a hermeneutics of the self, but rather an ethics of self-control and self-mastery.

The third volume, *The Care of the Self*, began with the discussion of Artemidorus' book *The Interpretation of Dreams*. It was no chance which led Foucault back to those scenes which had already played a decisive role in Freud's portrayals of psychoanalytical processes. Nevertheless, in Foucault's view, this prehistory of psychoanalysis was by no means the key to an anthropological understanding which attempted to emancipate man through a constant deciphering of his inward, enigmatic worlds. On the contrary, Foucault's *Traumdeutung* (dream interpretation) can be seen as a complete rejection of psychoanalytical hermeneutics of the dream. Foucault 'rehabilitated' the dream as the nocturnal mirror of the soul reflecting the fights and afflictions of the day rather than the nature of desire. Dream worlds consist of mood images, they are indicators for the individual's physical and mental make-up within the context of his concrete environment.

Foucault was interested in the techniques which, for the mastering of one's own life, elicited a long list of ethical problems; techniques which were not primarily determined by institutional constraints, but by the manner of relationship which one could have to oneself. Foucault did not see man's cultural conditions become apparent in a hermeneutical deciphering of the subject, but on the surface of a power struggle to be survived by the individual within life itself. Foucault's analysis of Artemidorus' *Interpretation of*

Dreams attempted to show that the dream illustrated, as a play upon its strengths and weaknesses, individual existence itself.

Artemidorus was concerned with the interpretation of everyday dreams. His book on dreams was a practical advisor, a 'handbook-for-daily-living' (CS 6), a tool assisting in conducting one's life. For Artemidorus, the dreamer was not a subject whose dreams provided information about a hidden life or any undiscovered identity. In the male-dominated Greek and Roman society of classical antiquity, the dreamer Artemidorus turned to was the man. It was therefore primarily a question of 'men's dreams', reflecting, in their concrete social context, commonplace cares.

Artemidorus was not trying to discover any universally valid functional connections of the human psyche which might be manifested in dreams. His dream interpretation concentrated on the needs of the male individual in the context of his everyday experiences. As the subject of the dream, this man was also the focal point of *The Interpretation of Dreams*. Artemidorus' book should assist the man's life and conduct, not the symbols which inhabit a dream. At the centre of Artemidorus' dream analysis was the individual's current state. In addition to that, the dream was part of a cosmic order, anticipating future events and reflecting the dreamer's hopes and fears. For in the dreamer's emotions, the day's work was anticipated or recapitulated; in them, the subject taking care of himself and his life had a 'language' which helped him in coping intuitively with the daily tasks of life, thus complementing reason.

In the place of mere dream analysis Foucault employed the term 'oneirocriticism' (dream criticism) (CS 14), intending to express the fact that an interpretation of dreams in Artemidorus' sense was primarily an instrument of a comprehensive life technique, a *technē tou biou*. For Foucault, Artemidorus' text was no evidence that a hermeneutics of the dream already existed in the second century AD. More than the phantasmagoria of a dream, the focal point was the subject dreaming of an act which, in Artemidorus, still coincided with the subject of the act.

A sexual dream, in which the dreamer himself is the main protagonist of sexual acts, was directly connected to the dreamer's real life. The dream, with its multi-faceted image-world, derived its concrete meaning, based on everyday life, from this unity between dream-subject and dreamer. Should the sleeper show himself erotic images, Artemidorus did not then enquire into the sexual nature of the dream, nor into *Verdrängungen* (repressions) appearing to suggest some hidden desire of the dreamer. Rather, the dream referred to the dreamer's social environment and to events which, in view of his respective social situation or employment, might still be in store for him. Foucault underlined here the 'ambiguity between the sexual meaning and the economic meaning of certain terms' (CS 27). 'Taking possession' of a woman or a boy sexually, could, in a dream, also refer to that affluence which one might be able to obtain in the near future.

As previously in the case of dietetics, the penetration model, representative of virile morals and described by Foucault in the preceding volume, the male member (*anagkaion*) also bore central significance in the double-meaning and ambiguity of the economic-sexual 'dream vocabulary'. As 'a man's book that is addressed mainly to men in order to help them lead their lives as men' (CS 28), Artemidorus' *Interpretation of Dreams* was also geared to a man's way of life. In this respect, the penetration model corresponded to the inner logic of a 'male dream'. For Artemidorus, masculinity was synonymous with the values of sexual potency and economic afflu-ence. There were no exclusive divisions in so far as both were important areas of life and as such laid claim to particular attention and caution.

Foucault interpreted Artemidorus' analysis of sexual dreams in a manner which for today's reader, familiar with psychoanalytical dream interpretation, appears superficial. In Artemidorus' time, social characteristics were far more important than the dreamer's past. Hence it is also to be understood why the significance of the dream figures lay not in their personality, but in the social status they occupied as compared with the dreamer: 'who penetrates whom' (CS 30) – that is the question.

Artemidorus' gauge for interpreting the relationships between the dream figures and the dreamer was the penetration act. Rather than being on the look-out for various polymorphous sexual prac-tices, which, in the dream's psychoanalytical language assisted in exposing the dreamer's desire, the predominant principle was the act of penetration structuring the social scenario and thus allowing its interpretation. At the same time, the act of penetration was, as an expression of the utmost masculine activity, the highest positive grade in Artemidorus' scale of values. The more inactive the dreamer, the more negative were the results of the dream interpre-tation for him. This applied not only to sexual pleasures, in which one assumed either the dominant role of penetrator or the submissive role of the penetrated; it was equally valid for life's economic aspect, which also functioned according to an undifferentiated either/or principle: either one attained profit, or one suffered a loss.

The sexual act and social status of the dreamer were interconnected and obeyed a 'rule of isomorphism' (CS 32). For a free man, penetrating a slave was a positive dream vision, since it corresponded to his social rank. Appearing in a dream, the penetration of a slave could be read isomorphically as an economic promise of prosperity. The sexual act acquired its significance, according to the rule of isomorphism established by Foucault, in the manner 'in which the dreaming subject maintains, as the subject of the dreamed-of act, his position as a social subject' (CS 33).

For Artemidorus, the key to dream interpretation was the male member. Its diverse virile characteristics established the link between dream vision and the dreamer's current existence, thus allowing the former's interpretation. The *anagkaion* not only symbolized the free man's superiority and legal rights, but also implied the necessity for self-control. The male member represented 'the subject's 'style of activity' (CS 35) in all spheres of daily conduct and their sovereign mastery.

For Foucault, Artemidorus' book reflected the continuity of virile ethics since the fourth century BC. It dealt with the moral problematization of a lifestyle which was constituted predominantly within a monosexual social structure. For this society the penetration model was the natural standard. Instead of a hidden archaeology of sexual pleasures, the male organ embodied the productive strength on the surface of being.

The basis for the ancient dream, however, is not male self-glorification in the sense of over-estimating oneself, but the proximity to social life and to the duties a man held within that life. In his analysis of *The Interpretation of Dreams*, Foucault was not showing the fixation on one's own sex and its glorification. Sexual activity, as revealed in the dream vision, was not interpreted in isolation through distracting 'sexual symbols', but as a part and representation of a way of life which was subject to the duties and constraints of an 'ethical virility' (UP 83). Artemidorus' book on dreams was above all a handbook for coping with life's daily tasks using dream analysis as an aid. The dream did not conceal some enigmatic self nor liberated a repressed desire whose secret sign was contained within the dream vision. It mirrored, rather, the current situation, thus giving the dreamer the opportunity to recognize conflicts and find a remedy according to the dream's interpretation. Artemidorus was no ancient code-worker but a sort of counsellor. This form of counselling did not apply, as was later the case with Freud, to bourgeois society and its sexual morphology, but to the virile life world, to which Artemidorus himself belonged. For him, the dream was an instrument for a technique of life, and not the scene of some urge to confess.

THE CULTIVATION OF THE SELF

Foucault detected shifts of emphasis within moral reflection which were significant for the second century AD: The pleasures were regarded with greater suspicion and increasing severity, and more consideration was given to their effects on body and soul. There was, furthermore, a stronger polarization between the marriage model and the love of boys: The former underwent a clearly perceptible valorization, while the latter no longer appeared to constitute the focal point of an erotic moral reflection, thus gradually forfeiting its social relevance, in particular as a pedagogical strategy. On the basis of the prescriptive texts of Rufus, Seneca, Plutarch, Epictetus and Marcus Aurelius, Foucault traced these changes, at the same time emphasizing their later influence on Christian moral history.

Central to the classical texts to which Foucault referred was the insistence on self-care. This intense self-relation was accompanied by an attitude towards the pleasures characterized by mistrust and caution. In these modifications concerning the previously analysed moral reflection of the fourth century BC, Foucault saw no historical 'rupture' between the Hellenistic and Roman epochs in which care of the self and the form of self-relation could be attributed to an intensification of private life. In his view there was, on the contrary, a continuity extending into the second century AD, 'of what might be called a "cultivation of the self", wherein the relations of oneself to oneself were intensified and valorized' (CS 43). In this sense, the third volume of The History of Sexuality is also to be seen as a continuation of the analysis of a culture of the self as it developed from fourth century BC Greece to its temporary historical climax in the Roman Empire of the second century AD. In this the term 'self-relation', at the highest level of a culture of the self, did not simply mean having an agonistic relationship to oneself in which one had to be stronger than oneself; rather it was, above and beyond this, 'the forms in which one is called upon to take oneself as an object of knowledge and a field of action, so as to transform, correct, and purify oneself, and find salvation' (CS 42).

An ethics, of which the fundamental principle is self-concern (and its problematized techniques of self-mastery), cannot be seen simply as the luxury of a temporary philosophical reflection, but must be understood as a principle inherent in the very culture of antiquity. Here Foucault did not define culture on the basis of institutional achievements or the functioning of state organizations; instead he sought to take an individually and physiologically directed ethical standard for the foundation and opportunity for culture itself. Only thus does it become clear why the theme of a culture of the self, so central to antiquity, was reflected as an art of existence. The fact that a pagan art of living, problematized in such a way, attained, in the first two centuries after Christ, 'a kind of golden age in the cultivation of the self' (CS 45), was not considered by Foucault as a euphemistic diagnosis of an historical epoch; rather, he saw it primarily as confirmation of a heyday for a culture of self-relation, reserved for an elite circle of free men. No more, however, was it his intention to consider, in the sense of modern social criticism, a minority at the top which formed, to an extent, the aristocratic caste in a slave society. For Foucault, care of the self (*epimeleia heautou, cura sui*), imparted by ancient culture, had central significance as the starting point for an art of living and a stylization of oneself. Foucault saw the prime task of his studies in the development of that care's ethical and moral bases.

For the philosophers and doctors of Hellenistic and Roman antiquity, care of the self was not a general principle of life, equally valid for everybody; instead, they turned to the individuals who wished 'to lead a life different from that of "the throngs"' (CS 40). In this respect, philosophy was the ethical effort of making one's own existence the focus of a care which served in the arrangement and stylization of life's daily tasks. It was the attempt not to leave one's own being to the contingent course of fate, but to allow it, through the preservation and intensification of self-relation, to become an intentional work of an as yet unformed life.

In his reflections on the brevity of life (*De brevitate vitae*), Seneca's expression *se formare* defined the pivotal thought in a stylization of one's own existence. If Seneca was philosophizing, then it was in the sense that he took time for himself; the value of the philosophical exercise lay in taking care of himself, and in reflecting on the demands and the possible order of the day-to-day obligations of life. A constant care revolved around one's own being, a care which at the same time was founded in the instinctive knowledge that culture altogether only becomes possible through the act of 'self-endeavour'. Thus for Seneca and other Stoics, the preoccupation with oneself was not the mere expression of a pastime in which one indulged oneself on the periphery of social obligations; nor even a narcissistic contemplation of one's own ego, which would have been representative for the vanities of an elite. 'It is a valuable principle for everyone, all the time and throughout life' (CS 48).

Foucault was here describing a use of philosophy which was fundamentally different from its present institutionalized form. Instead of being primarily an object of academic specialist knowledge, pedagogically legitimized by the state as a university faculty, philosophy in antiquity was first and foremost connected to the question as to which knowledge was possible as far as an art of an individually adjusted way of life was concerned. In this respect, the scandal for modern philosophy which Foucault provoked with his analysis of self-relations and self-techniques is the wish, far from a hermeneutical will to know, that a person should take care of himself 'as perhaps the most important matter with which he could be concerned' (CS 48). Cultivating care of the self means making oneself the highest precept of a philosophical way of life. Foucault saw the central theme of a culture of the self not in the academic appropriation of philosophical knowledge – which ultimately reduces philosophy to philosophical-historical contents – nor in a philosophical-ethical doctrine which might issue universally valid rules for a way of life; he saw it rather in the objective of taking oneself, one's body, and one's soul as the material for a beautiful lifework.

'Help yourself if your soul's salvation is dear to you', runs an imperative of Marcus Aurelius. In this reversal of Christian ethics, for which altruism and self-renunciation, as elements of worldly morality, were deemed necessary for the claim to divine promise of salvation in the hereafter, Aurelius saw each person's placing in life as an *amor fati*: The responsibility which one bore towards one's own life had to be accompanied by a care of the self all the greater, the more the danger existed of forfeiting one's earthly salvation through self-neglect. To prevent this, the care of the self was a question of exercise in which the perils of life were to be resisted. Body and soul had to be 'kept in form' throughout one's life.

Foucault pointed out that the targets of this call to self-care were no longer the still immature boys given lessons by Socrates, but this time, in the second century, grown men. An *Erwachsenenerziehung* (adult education) had now developed from an education of boys (*paidika*) – a pedagogy based on love of boys. This reveals the extent to which the boy's former antinomy as one-time central aspect of an ethical problematic appears to have lost significance; instead, there began to emerge a symmetry already demanded by Plato but until then unattained, in which truth became the structuring element. For in a culture of the self, with free, adult men as its bearers, access to the truth was the same for everyone. It was no longer the discrepancy between *erastes* as the master and the *eromenos* as the youth commended to him which was the focal point of philosophical reflection, and which portrayed an apparently insuperable paradox; rather it was the relationship one could have with the truth by taking care of oneself.

As in *The Use of Pleasure*, here too Foucault emphasized the gearing of ancient lifestyle, as yet untainted by the Christian morality of self-renunciation, towards the requirements of *this* world. Ancient ethics concentrated on the mastering of daily life through oneself, on the styling and best possible balance of that life. One paid attention to one's body, devoting care to it according to the respective circumstances and situations of life, keeping it healthy with sensible nutrition. The body was toughened with physical exercises, and care was taken that the body's needs were satisfied in moderation. In order to submit to these exercises and regulations, necessary and useful for both body and soul, a seclusion with oneself was indispensable. Through an attitude of constant consultation with oneself one had to preserve the ability to recall the general bases for a correct way of life. However, Foucault perceived this self-relation, which gave rise to ancient behaviour, not as an egoistic or narcissistic phenomenon; it was 'not an exercise in solitude, but a true social practice' (CS 51).

The direct concern for the self went hand in hand with a duty of care towards others. This was not fixed institutionally, as is characteristic in many areas of today's society, and in which, among others, teachers, psychologists and doctors exercise important functions of general counselling. In contrast to this functional divi-

sion and distribution of counselling which has been acquired by
modern societies, in the Hellenistic world 'the interplay of the care
of the self and the help of the other' (CS 53) was not tied to single
institutions or their representatives: 'in the practice of the cultivation of the self, the roles were often interchangeable, and they
could be played in turn by the same person' (CS 52).

Here Foucault brought to light the virtualities of a culture
opposed to modern mass society. Compared with the reductional-
ist dominance and power of modern institutions and their social
spheres of influence, the advising functions of teacher and doctor
in Seneca's time were far less bound to persons legitimized by institutions; they revealed themselves rather on the basis of
many-layered relationships. The rhetorical and literary testimonies
of the Hellenistic era which Foucault referred to reflected in what
variable manner 'the work of oneself on oneself and communication with others were linked together' (CS 51). Not the authority of
'professionals of spiritual direction' (CS 52) – which modern
language usage terms psychoanalysts – guaranteed the physical
and spiritual salvation of the individual. Through a tracing back of
the institutions to a culture of the self, Foucault was attempting to
show the diversity of relationships which arose within the
individual's relationship, on the one hand to his own body and
soul, and on the other, to his fellow individuals. Foucault paid
particular attention to the situative variability, adapting to life
circumstances of relationships, which were not necessarily linked
to institutions. In his view there lay here the building block for an
ancient culture of the self, not yet caught up by the development
towards greater social unity, in which reglemented institutions
became necessary.

'COUNTER-ALEXANDERS': PLEASURE IN ONESELF[1]

Body and soul, those parts of human nature which need and
complement each other, were reflected in the medicine and philosophy of the Roman-Hellenistic epoch. Moral reflection had its
starting point here. In contrast to their later separation, medicine
and philosophy still formed a mutual cooperation and juxtaposition which was also apparent in the customary terminology of
the time. Thus 'the concept of "pathos"' (CS 54) played a crucial
role for both disciplines. In antiquity, 'pathos' did not yet have

the nosographic meaning of a pathology as it did for medicine in the nineteenth century, but applied, on a less specific level, to a 'disturbance' of physical and mental functions. Foucault interpreted this affinity between medicine and morals as being a greater care and anxiety expressed towards the body. In this sense he quoted Epictetus: 'The philosopher's school is a physician's consulting-room' (CS 55). The reason for this increasing care lay not least in the fact that it was no longer the boy's developing body which was the central object of moral interest, but the body of a grown man. Thus there arose a shift in emphasis away from the modelling of the boy's young physique towards the general susceptibility of the man's mature body. Henceforth, there appeared to be a greater danger emanating from the fragility of the body than from the soul itself. Following the intensity of a philosophical moral reflection was an increasing 'medicinization' in the manner in which one guarded one's soul.

Attentiveness towards body and soul logically compels a knowledge of oneself. The Delphic oracle here discernible does not refer solely to its association with Socrates, but rather gives validity to general physiological principles. One should practice keeping in mind the actual basic requirements of body and soul, and forgoing all luxury and non-essentials. Sovereignty in this context also means being able to 'free' oneself from one's property, to renounce it in situations where one does well to own oneself, instead of being 'possessed' by one's property. This referred not only to one's personal belongings, but also to natural needs; to fulfil them beyond the necessary limit was tantamount to a restriction of one's own sovereignty, for an excessive satisfaction of needs tended to increase rather than still the desire for them.

Inherent in the daily practical exercises was a permanent need for self-correction, which if necessary should steer excess and lack back to their natural limit. Eating and drinking was to be done in moderation. Taking Seneca once more as his example, Foucault showed how the former reviewed the day gone by and accounted for his accomplishments and omissions. By recalling a finished day Seneca re-checked the correctness or error of his actions. His corrective daily inventory was to enable him to discover what should be changed in his actions. In Foucault's opinion, such an inspection of oneself was not, as he probably demonstrated for Christianity in the unpublished sequel volume *Les Aveux de la Chair* (*The Confessions of the Flesh*), a confessional of daily sins. Nor was a legal relationship expressed in it, as is the case in a categoric observance of laws. In his daily exercises and inventories, Seneca was not concerned with accumulating a guilt which testified to a possible moral reprehensibility in his life. In the foreground of his behaviour was the work of reason and its intrinsic ability for self-correction. Only reason guaranteed the user sovereignty through the possibility of restrictive measures. In this activity reason was shown to be 'the necessity of a labor of thought with itself as object' (CS 62), which concentrated on 'a constant attitude that one must take toward oneself' (CS 63). With this, Foucault meant an activity of incessant self-examination, a testing of oneself which should ensure both the use of power within a rationally directed self-constitution and the securing of one's own freedom. One's perceptions should always be checked and weighed against the relationship to one's self.

Foucault's greatest interest in ancient culture, the crux of his studies on a history of sexuality, can be summarized succinctly in the following Greek words: 'Epistrophē eis heauton'. With this the 'general principle of conversion to self' (CS 64) is defined. This does not mean that the daily obligations of one's profession and other spheres of life should be neglected in favour of an idle preoccupation with oneself, but that precisely these obligations should be met on account of oneself, 'that the chief object one should set for oneself is to be sought within oneself, in the relation of oneself to oneself' (CS 64–5). In his final studies, Foucault was interested neither in the disciplining power of institutions, nor in the duty of obedience to the law, nor in the state's power of disposal over individuals, nor in the normative effect of discourses; rather, he was concerned with an irreducible self-relation of the individuum which could be comprehended not theoretically, but as an aesthetical phenomenon of a complicated lifework.

The goal of the self-practices was not a different life, nor one in the hereafter; they did not serve to prepare a person for such a life through cleansing. Instead they applied to the relationship which one assumed, or could assume, with oneself and one's life. To look after oneself and to be one's own object of joy was the telos of a culture of the self, a complete life experience which in the here-and-now acclaimed the self as the most precious of possessions. In an ethics of self-concern 'Know thyself!' was complemented by 'Please yourself, learn joy in yourself!'

The ancient self analysed by Foucault is not the Freudian unconscious with its hidden depths, nor is it the idle self, draped in the vain robes of Narcissus and remaining apart from any genital organization; rather it is a state – inaccessible to theoretical fixing – which 'arises out of ourselves and within ourselves' (CS 66). The self is, as it were, the splendour of an existence, the centrepiece of an ethical activity. It is the particular and personal work of self-cultivation in which one ultimately takes pleasure. Foucault compared man's supposedly transcendental essence with pagan ethics in which one was simultaneously the subject of one's actions, and the object of a pleasure in oneself. This ethics of self-concern found its highest expression in an aesthetics of existence.

The difference which Foucault saw between the fourth century BC and the heyday of a culture of the self within pagan ethics in the first centuries AD, lay in a shift of attention from ascetics to self-knowledge. It was no longer so much the exercises necessary for continence towards the pleasures which were central to the question of how one constituted oneself as moral subject, but the relationship which one had to the truth – 'the truth concerning what one is, what one does, and what one is capable of doing' (CS 68). This truth about oneself by virtue of self-knowledge structured the relationship to oneself. In this relationship, however, a far greater importance was attached to action than to knowledge. Truth in this case therefore, did not mean the quantity of knowledge but a work of thought on oneself; thought which should not be clouded by following the rules, but one in which the focus of attention was the ethical work. This alone created access to a self-knowledge which did not dwell on the mere discovery of oneself, but which claimed to model, through various modifications, a work from the material of one's life.

Foucault was describing a time in which the subject of desire was not yet in existence – in contrast to later Christianity, which was to 'continue' pagan ethics under changed conditions, and which led to the hermeneutic subject of desire. The pagan 'subject' central to the culture of the self analysed by Foucault was a man of action who gauged himself and his strengths in the course of his daily activities, and who stylized himself as moral subject through a work on himself. He was himself the object of a *joie de vivre*, and not the subject of a desire. The 'Foucauldian subject' appears on the surface of 'Freudian inwardness'; it does not sublimate, it acts.

POLITICS AS ETHOS

In the Graeco-Roman world of the first two centuries AD, the constitution of oneself as the ethical subject of one's own actions took on
problematic traits. Marriage experienced stronger 'publicizing' (CS
73), leading to greater attention being paid to the wife's role; consequently, neither did the man's self-relation remain untouched by
this new moral quality. With regards to political relations, characterized by the progressing dissolution of the city states, a general
redistribution of power practice began to emerge. With the
growing complexity of the Roman administration an increasing
functionalization of power took place, particularly reflected in the
demand for a 'service aristocracy' ('managerial aristocracy') (CS 84).
According to Foucault, the political and social changes within the
Roman world did not cause any turning away from a culture of the
self, but rather impeled its intensification.

Foucault rejected those attempts at interpretation which saw in
the increase of civic duties a supposed retreat into 'private life'. In
his view the intensification of self-concern was, on the contrary, an
indication of the reciprocity between public and private milieu.
Thus Foucault saw no conflict between a political life taking place
in public and a private life led in seclusion; he emphasized rather
the manner in which both spheres were ethically related to each
other. The relationship between an individual and his political
activity embraced an entire sphere of action.

The individual's action and political role were not legitimized
solely by social status: the one who 'exercises power has to place
himself in a field of complex relations where he occupies a transi-
tion point' (CS 88). Therefore, Foucault's portrayal of Hellenistic
politics is inseparable from a stylistics of existence; the politics of
the Empire era is distinguished precisely by the individual acting in
public. Unlike the case of present-day professionals, where even
politics is specialized and political activity is reserved above all for
the so-called 'professional politicians [*Berufspolitiker*]'[2] who represent a particular part of social values, the politics of that time was
still an ethos which included the moral demand to be able first to
govern oneself, in order to be worthy of governing and leading
others. 'The rationality of the government of others is the same as
the rationality of the government of oneself' (CS 89). In this, it was
not obedience to the law which guaranteed one's own sovereignty,
but the, as it were, 'playful' constitution of oneself, linked to reason.

Thus here too, preoccupation with the self formed the inalienable prerequisite for a political life: A man must 'guide his own soul, establish his own *ēthos*' (CS 89).

At this point it becomes clear how much Foucault's original intention of analysing a modern 'bio-power' (HS 140) differs from the description of an ancient subject who attempted to create the malleable material of his existence from his own *bios*. For Foucault, the focal point in this was reason, as the most important instrument of ethical activity; for it was reason's task to limit the use of power and prevent its tendency to hubris and the misuse which can result from this. In his final studies, Foucault's glance rested not on the regimented 'bio-power' of the modern state, but on the possibility of a tempered existence of the individual. In this respect his attempt to develop a culture of the self from the example of antiquity can also be seen as an exposure of cultural virtualities arising in part outside the state order, and without the institutions responsible for the majority of democratic social structures. Such a culture is undemocratic in the original Greek sense, because it is not a popular culture but addresses those individuals who consider an ethics of self-care and an aesthetics of existence to be worth striving for. In antiquity, those individuals were the free men. The potential connection to the present which Foucault bore in mind here will be explained at a later stage.

Ethos, for Foucault's interpretation of a culture of the self, was 'the individual's "retreat within himself"' (CS 91), which depended on a relationship to oneself and an ethical work on oneself. The modelling of oneself was in a reciprocal and isomorphic relationship to the modelling of political work. In this reciprocity, Foucault particularly stressed the personal commitment of the individual who, as moral subject of himself, gained validity and recognition beyond his status, and was uninfluenced by the limitations of his prescribed legal ability to act. In one of his last lectures, Foucault also termed this commitment 'truth-telling'.

In the light of his studies on antiquity, Foucault's concept of power broke away from its institutional context. He problematized power from its individual use and from the attitude which the individual assumed in consideration of his own natural limits. The development of the self-constituting moral subject took into account his entire circumstances of life, thus creating a stylistics of existence unique to him, and in which political life was also integrated as an aspect of ethical activity. In this sense, 'heautocratism'

(CS 95) denoted not merely the form of self-relation but the very problematic of its ethical implementation. Foucault thus described the problematic of the subject's self-mastery – long before that subject became a servant of the state.

THE BODY'S REASON

In the Graeco-Roman world, medicine was still very far removed from the 'hospital industry' of the modern age with its comprehensive nosography and the to some degree complementary pharmaceutical industry. In place of a gigantic organization caring for the public health, medicine in antiquity was a life practice; it was 'a way of living, a reflective mode of relation to oneself, to one's body, to food' (CS 100). Medicine had the task, not of trusting to the outside help of specialists, but of taking care of one's own health with the aid of dietetics and one's reason. Medicine as equipment of life meant firstly 'to be one's own health counsellor' (CS 100). In this respect medical knowledge and dietetics were a life technique which one employed without having to constantly obtain a doctor's advice. In his analysis, Foucault emphasized that the ancient concern for the susceptibility of the body and the preservation of its health assumed a central place in an ethics of self-concern. It was only from this viewpoint that the dealing with sexual pleasures was problematized and the ancient theme of the correct regimen continued; a theme which, compared with the *aphrodisia*, formed a more important object of moral reflection.

Using Galen as an example, Foucault attempted to describe the relation to the pleasures in the Hellenistic epoch and to determine their place within moral reflection. In contrast to earlier centuries there was an alteration regarding a greater care for the 'pathological concomitants' of the pleasures. The concept of the pathological still had little affinity to the modern one, but already the tendency to give the pleasures a negative connotation was becoming apparent. For the pleasures were increasingly suspected of being a source of the body's liability to weakness. Thus the man as 'the spermatic animal par excellence' (CS 112) was confronted with the problem that a precious part of his body, the semen, was lost through the sexual act. This 'pathological effect' of the sexual act was particularly symbolized in the idea of priapism or satyriasis, which revealed the hubris inherent in the pleasures, and it was therefore considered advisable as far as possible to abstain from coitus.

Here too, Foucault showed the little significance attached to the quality of sexual activity, and the extent to which, in a pagan ethics of correct temperance, that activity was judged on its quantity. In this light the second century AD did not differ essentially from the preceding centuries; what had changed however, in relation to the pleasures, was the now more strongly considered vulnerability of the body. It was no longer the techniques of the self for the mastery of one's forces which stood central in the moral eye, but the fragile body.

In his unpublished sequel volume, *Les Aveux de la Chair*, Foucault would have tried to show how the scepticism of this view gradually transformed into a Christian morality, in which the pleasures underwent a noticeable defamation. Nevertheless he warned against interpreting the concern of this view as being already the harbinger of the Christian era. The care of protecting the body still belonged to a pagan culture of the self which took a closer look at the body, whose living presence outweighed denunciation of the flesh in the name of an 'omnipotent father'.

Foucault differentiated four aspects of pagan moral reflection for which a dietetic dealing with the *aphrodisia* appeared necessary, and in which the regime of the pleasures should be approached with a restrictive economy: The moment of procreation, age, time of the day or year, and the individual temperament. Important for begetting descendants was not correct 'family planning' but above all that one 'must form oneself as the prior image of the child one wishes to have' (CS 125). One should be in a good state physically and mentally at the moment of procreation, for 'the embryo will be imbued with the condition of the procreators' (CS 126). Furthermore, in order to beget strong, healthy descendants, intercourse should not be indulged in at untimely moments. For the choice of the correct moment for procreation, various precautionary measures were considered, but the most important object of concern was oneself: Only by taking responsibility for oneself was one considered worthy of having descendants. The care with which one made the decision to have children was simultaneously a care of one's own general state.

In the question of possible age limitations too, a rationally orientated conduct corresponding to the respective time of life and those changing physical needs and state of health was to be considered.

Dietetic and physical exercises were held necessary for young people, in order for them to resist the temptation to early sexual intercourse, and to pay attention to their own health. It was a general but non-binding advice, that neither in very early years nor in one's latter days, should one succumb to sexual pleasures beyond one's limit, so as to maintain as healthy a state as possible in accordance with the fragility and frailty of age. However, even here, the demand for abstinence did not aim at declaring the *aphrodisia* a 'taboo zone', but rather at mastering their use, according to one's age, with the help of exercises on oneself.

Attention to a particular regimen applied fundamentally to the correct moment (*kairos*) in which one could succumb to the *aphrodisia*. Nutritional composition should take into account the different seasons and times of day; at the same time, diet was an important criteria for the use of the pleasures. It was not the form of pleasure, nor the excessiveness of a desire, but precisely the exercise of moderation as a rule of health, which gave both digestion and its dietetic requirements a similarity to coitus. In an ethics of existence, in which care of the self had central place, attention to the body's regimen began with the external and internal dangers which threatened it. Far from the modern overrating of the sexual and the formation of identity ascribed to it, in ancient moral reflection dealings with the pleasures were a part of a more comprehensive conception of life, in which mastery of one's self still had precedence over a 'sexual liberation'.

Foucault's selected texts reveal the extent to which the ancients cared about maintaining the balance between the body's susceptible constitution and what was healthy for it with respect to the *aphrodisia*. If one disregarded this balance by ignoring the dietetic regulations, one ran the risk of bringing the body's regimen out of its natural equilibrium. It was not a question of some secret desire which had to be discovered; rather it was the fundamentally jeopardized body which necessitated an almost meticulous concern for physiology. 'It is as if the body dictated to the body' (CS 133).

The main focus, however, was applied not exclusively to the body and the questions regarding a correct diet, but also to the work which one had to carry out on the soul and the passions it radiated. Body and soul stood in a balanced relation to one another, so that the steering of the soul allowed those laws to be observed which corresponded to the physiological dynamics of the body. Physical regimen went hand in hand with a moral regimen, which was to prevent the soul's desire from exceeding the physical desire. In antiquity, the relation between body and soul, which in later Christianity developed into an antagonism, was a tension field in which the common denominator was the natural need. The naturalness of a need could be gauged and understood through the body itself. If the natural limit was exceeded, dysfunctions could occur resulting in a threat to one's own existence. 'Natural' here means, therefore, recognizing the boundaries set by nature and harmonizing one's own life with them both physically and spiritually, through the moderate application of natural powers and needs. In this context, Rufus' apparently paradoxical formular quoted by Foucault can be understood: 'subdue the soul and make it obey the body' (CS 135). One had to listen to the needs of one's body, for those needs reflected a rationality inherent in the natural order itself. The body functions according to an economy which is intrinsic to life and which is determined by the interplay of 'intake' and 'output'. According to this natural law, the soul had also to fulfil its duty of care towards the body, and banish those passions which threatened to increase unnecessarily desire for the *aphrodisia*. The 'ancient soul' was subject to the natural laws which upheld the body's functions; its 'salvation' depended on the observance of those laws, and not on obedience to a religiously endowed meaning over and above nature.

The previously established juxtaposition of digestion and sexual pleasure by which Foucault exemplified the basic economic principle, indicated a 'seismographic' function of the body, whose signals were to be interpreted by the soul with the greatest of care. For Foucault's interpretation, an 'ethics of desire' was linked to a 'philosophy of excretions'. It was 'the tendency toward an ideal point where the soul, purified of all its vain representations, no longer gives its attention to anything but the austere economy of organic functions' (CS 136). In Foucault's analysis of ancient moral reflection, modern hermeneutics of desire was opposed to an ethics grounded in physiology. In his opinion, the ancient striving for a temperate lifestyle which ascertained correct limits was here substantiated; a lifestyle which, from lack of that self-care necessary for such an ethics, was to be lost for a long time.

Foucault also dealt with that gesture of solitary cleansing which, beyond the problematic use of the pleasures, is 'an act of natural elimination, which has the value both of a philosophical lesson and a necessary remedy' (CS 140). What is meant is masturbation as the self-sufficing act of nature. It was not without irony that Foucault referred to Diogenes, for whom masturbation was 'an act that, done in time, would have made the Trojan War unnecessary' (CS 140). These references however, are not directed polemically at the advocates of a functionally related genital organization, who, in a ranking of sexual pleasures, viewed such a gesture of self-concern as inferior. For a culture of the self in which one constitutes oneself as moral subject on the strength of one's reason, masturbation is the most rational act; it is the individual's pleasure in himself. Since the source of the pleasure lies in the individual himself, he can also be an object of (sexual) enjoyment. To have delight in oneself – that is the aesthetic quintessence, not searching for meaning, of an ethics of self-concern, valid to the same extent for the self-sufficient act of masturbation.

In this section of his interpretation, Foucault had tried to show how conspicuously the role of nutritional dietetics stood out in Greek and Roman medicine in comparison to that of sexual pleasures. The pleasures could, just as much as false nutrition, lead to a jeopardizing of the individual's physical and spiritual equilibrium, and thus required permanent inspection. It was not the infinitely striving desire which formed the core of attention, but the constant awareness of those rules which allowed sexual activity to be limited and controlled. To find the rules within oneself, according to which the art of a moderated existence develops; to recognize within oneself the physiological basis for one's own rationality was, for Foucault's analysis of pagan ethics, the starting point for a rational way of life and an art of self-stylization.

LIFESTYLES IN CONFLICT

The Universality of Marriage

Through Xenophon's *Oeconomicus*, Foucault tried to show marriage's significance for the fourth century BC. Essentially it was defined by the man's ability to master himself and his wife within the order of the household. Nonetheless, in the time of the Roman Empire, this virile role of leadership was changing: The former asymmetry between the marriage partners increasingly gave way to a symmetry which enhanced the status both of the wife and of marriage itself, drawing it more into the public sphere. Instead of the husband's one-sided leadership, the partners were connected by 'a "marriage tie"' (CS 150) beyond the previously untouched juridical form of marriage, in which the wife was allocated a firm place as mistress of the house and servant of her husband.

Marriage should no longer be legitimized solely by the reproductive function, but should also gain greater weight through an affective bond between the partners. From knowledge of the natural order, which united man and wife for the purpose of preserving the species, there arose an understanding of man as a conjugal being, which formed the core and ultimately the authorization of the couple's relationship. In addition, marriage was 'one of those duties by which private existence acquires a value for all' (CS 155). In this demand for universality, however, it was not a question of social consensus. There was disagreement between those who regarded marriage as incompatible with a philosophically conducted existence, and those who considered the integration of marriage within a philosophically led existence as exemplary. The philosopher's celibacy and the demand for the universality of marriage would no longer apply, 'if all humans were in a condition to lead an existence conforming to their essential nature' (CS 159). But this ideal remained unattained in light of increasing concern for the woman during the period of the Roman Empire. More and more, marriage was problematized for both partners as an art of living together, a style of existence.

Although its valorization awakens the impression that marriage might have suppressed the culture of the self, it was nevertheless at first only part of a comprehensive technique of existence which was intended to master conjugal living. As such marriage remained integrated within a culture of the self. It is true that the marital bond was no longer characterized by that functional relationship of Xenophon's time; but despite matrimony's affective valorization, the relationship between the sexes was still determined by the paradox that the man's privileged position was untouched by the woman's valorization as wife. Conjugal unity was simply no longer reflected solely from the point of view of the man's self-knowledge, but found new value through the inclusion of the wife's position. This original paradox in the philosophical reflection on marriage was to be replaced by later Christianity with an insoluble and consecrated lifelong communion between man and wife, tolerating no other forms of relationship. Woman and man received their 'equality before God'. Right up to the present day, the monopoly of the Christian marriage has remained powerful and evident in almost every social sphere.

For the Stoics, on the other hand, a culture of the self was not accompanied by the demand for marriage. Preferring married life to celibacy did not mean a man should no longer take care of himself, but that the new art should henceforward consist of giving 'his married life a deliberate form and a particular style' (CS 163). The second century AD ethical and moral valorization of the marital bond did not at first affect sexual relations between the partners. Foucault referred to the fact 'that in the classical texts the synthesis of the marriage tie and sexual relations was granted mainly for reasons pertaining to procreation' (CS 166). Nevertheless, in the question of reciprocity of sexual activity within the context of an increasingly strict morality of marriage, there was also a 'conjugal-ization'. Even so, this demand did not result from any reprehensibility in the sexual pleasures with which Christianity was later to authorize marriage as the exclusive sphere of sexual practice. Opposed to the later sinfulness of the *aphrodisia* was the ethical argument that marriage be protected as that social organi-zation which could give 'man's existence ... its rational form' (CS 170).

The ethical grounds for marriage in Stoic morality originated in the rational and natural structure of the marital bond between man and woman as conjugal beings. From this viewpoint – and not for reasons of reprehensibility – the increasing severity in imposing a 'matrimonial limit' to sexual activities can also be understood. Along with the legally fixed demand for conjugal fidelity – which was nevertheless a far cry from the modern understanding of equality – the symmetry of affective fidelity formed a further basis for a stricter morality of marriage, turning the conjugal bond into a system 'that establishes an exact balance of obligations in the prac-tice of pleasure' (CS 173). In Foucault's opinion, such a demand for a reciprocal conjugalization was limited to Musonius' morality of marriage and could not be seen as representative for the Imperial period as a whole. Marriage as a variant of a stylistics of existence was not subjected to the authority of a written law according to which both partners would be equally obliged to submit them-selves. This also applied to the demand for mutual fidelity between the spouses which – in spite of growing symmetry – was by no means compulsory for both parties.

As he had for pre-Christian Greece, Foucault also observed for the Roman Era a noticeable silence regarding sexual pleasure within marriage. The reason lay in the greater attention to correct and moderate use of the *aphrodisia* within married life, and not – as would be symptomatic for the present – in the morphology of the pleasures between man and woman. People should not perform the act on account of its pleasurableness, but rather from the natural need to propagate one's species. A further reason applied to marriage as a 'fusion of existences' (CS 179) which, through the use of the pleasures solely within matrimony, promoted the community of the marital partners. In this the nature of sexual union is secondary, nor does marriage – as in Christianity – become an ideational unity between man and woman. It was primarily the production of progeny and the attempt to give the relationship between marriage and sexual activity 'a natural, rational, and essential' (CS 183) unity, which determined the most important problematizations of marriage and their affective valorization of the marital bond.

In spite of moral efforts to establish a greater symmetry between the spouses, the man's privileged position remained untouched. His role as husband was not defined solely by the conjugal bond with his wife but rather was to be harmonized with his relationship to himself. Far removed from the later institutionalization of marriage in the Christian pastoral – continued in its broad characteristics even in modern marriage laws – Foucault showed through the example of antiquity that marriage was no binding legal institution; rather it represented 'a mode of being, a style of relations' (CS 184), whose rules were of a general and not a compulsory nature which should serve all 'those who wish to give their existence an honourable and noble form. It is the lawless universality of an aesthetics of existence that in any case is practiced only by a few' (CS 185).

Despite this very different significance of the Hellenistic marriage to current matrimonial practice, the growing trend of its valorization could already be clearly recognized. It was precisely in those preferences ascribed to marriage that Foucault saw the parallel discrimination of the love of boys. The strengthening of the marriage institution, which preceded the later codification of behaviour forms, increasingly absorbed those practices of a culture of the self through which the individual showed himself to be responsible for his own existence.

The Virtue of Love of Boys

Parallel to a more rigid morality of marriage, Foucault observed for the first two centuries AD a 'deproblematization' (CS 189) of the love of boys. Although still well established in the Roman male-dominated society and considered as the natural pleasure and right of the adult man, the love of boys was overshadowed by a new perception of it as a moral problem, and thus forced more and more into the background. Not least the valorization of marriage and the waning significance of friendship between men had considerably weakened the once intensive philosophical reflection on the love of boys. Problematization of the pleasures was increasingly transferred to marriage, so that the former Socratic theme lost its relevance to the love of boys. 'This is the paradox: it was around the question of pleasure that reflection on pederasty developed in Greek antiquity; it is around this same question that it will go into decline' (CS 192). If the love of boys at one time formed the core of a stylistics of existence, it was subsequently marriage which, to an even greater extent, absorbed the delicate theme of love of boys and the integration of its pleasure.

Using three representative authors (Plutarch, Pseudo-Lucian, Maximus of Tyre), Foucault attempted to show how the significance of love of boys would be suppressed by the marriage model, even though the more clearly perceptible argument for the love of women drew on the ethics of the love of boys. Foucault described this seemingly paradoxical transformation, 'which confers on the relationship with a woman the same ethical potential as the relationship with a man' (CS 197). The wife should replace the *eromenos* in a more extensive form, and justify pleasure within the framework of marriage. Foucault furthermore illustrated how this transformation from the Eros of the love of boys to the Eros of love towards women led to the beginning of a distinction between homo- and heterosexuality – and ultimately to today's 'differential structure of desire' (CS 198).

In this way, Foucault's genealogical recourse to antiquity was also applicable to the specific elements of a moral reflection which were paving the way for a 'unification of erotics' (CS 199). The consequence of this unification was not, as yet, a division into homo- and heterosexual desire, since moral reflection in the second century AD did not have any uniform conception of sexuality and hence ruled out any differentiation of desire. In this respect modern concepts like 'homosexuality' or 'heterosexuality' are inadequate for the analysis of the most important differences between marriage and pederasty in antiquity. At least they do not contribute to the understanding of a culture for which the question of desire was integrated into the activity of an ethical work on oneself and its moderating attitude towards the pleasures. In antiquity, the problem was the integration of the pleasures and not the deciphering of the desire.

The discussion between the lovers of women on the one hand and the advocates of love of boys on the other, should not, then, be misconstrued as an argument on the subject of 'homo- or heterosexuality', nor as a question of tolerance. Contention centred rather on the *aphrodisia's* ability to integrate. Socrates' ascetic ideal which emerged from the asymmetry between *erastes* and *eromenos* should now find its apparently rational place within the institutional framework of matrimony. The ideal of virtue (*aretē*) traditional for the love of boys, as well as the often invoked friendship between *erastes* and *eromenos*, should now receive a new form from marriage, thus losing their former exclusivity within an erotics based on boys. This transformation became especially apparent with regards to moderation. The ascetic idea of moderation once formed the basis for the relationship between lover and beloved, only later finding equal significance in the conjugal bond. Moderation, which had to create an ethical foundation in the relationship between the *erastes* and his *eromenos* in place of the legitimate marital form, ultimately became the precondition for a symmetrical connection between the man and his wife. For it was the moderation principle which was equally required of both.

With the example of Plutarch, Foucault showed how those virtues, previously extolled for the erotics of boys, underwent their transfer to the marriage state. Plutarch's main argument against love of boys was its lack of grace (*charis*). On the basis of a natural polarity between the sexes, the woman's grace towards the man expressed general agreement. The wife's expression of goodwill was of weight in Plutarch's argumentation, and increasingly suppressed the complex love game between *erastes* and *eromenos*. The wife's *charis* in the marital bond surmounted the paradox of the devotion expected from the boy in the love act. Instead of the ascetic virtue of erotics of boys, forgoing the *aphrodisia* as much as possible in order not to injure the boy's honour, marriage seemed to allow the better integration and above all a reciprocity of the pleasures. The *charis* lacking in the love of boys due to its asymmetries (the boy's passivity, the lover's age difference, and the excluded reciprocity of loving) permitted in matrimony 'the internal regulation and the stability of the couple' (CS 209), and became in Plutarch the cornerstone of a new stylistics of love.

In a further text discussed by Foucault – Pseudo-Lucian's *The Affairs of the Heart* – the same problem is shown from a different perspective: it is concerned less with the integration of the sexual pleasures in the marital relationship than with 'the confrontation of two forms of life, of two ways of stylizing one's pleasure' (CS 218). In this contrast between two forms of existence, love of boys gained the esteem of a culture which went beyond nature, residing in this culture together with philosophy. Just as philosophy was seen as a manner of reflecting and mastering one's own life, so the Eros of the love of boys simultaneously allowed one to give truth a beautiful, transferable form. The art of married life, on the other hand, reflected by the Stoics, emphasized the necessity of a shared unity given by nature itself, which found adequate form in the marriage tie. In this the continuity and rationality of nature were decisive arguments for the love of women. The boy, however, lost his erotic value with his first beard, announcing his development into a free man, thus 'depreciating' the relationship between same sex lovers. The woman retained those physical characteristics which the boy lost as his body hair grew and his muscles became more pronounced. The Stoic plea for love of women found a further motive in the 'community of affection' (CS 219) between man and woman. The reciprocal exchange of sensuality between marriage partners conferred a natural legitimation on their bond beyond the boy's merely passive role as love- and pleasure-object of his suitor. Woman's natural passivity and devotion in the regimen of pleasures thus formed the basis for the moral justification of marriage in contrast to a boy debased in the act by his lover, and whose subservient attitude was condemned by lovers of women.

In Pseudo-Lucian's moral reflection, the greatest challenge for the supporters of pederasty was the *charis* which stressed the reciprocity of pleasure between partners of different sexes. Pederasts saw in virtue the common bond between the same sex lovers which outlasted pleasure itself. They countered the argument of the unnaturalness of pederasty with the cosmetic deception of the woman who did not reveal her true nature to the man, thus styling herself the source of a 'false' pleasure. For Foucault, the reason for this accusation lay particularly in the division of Hellenist society into a woman's and a man's world, in which both sexes pursued their own activities. This social rift made it possible to disqualify 'women as mysterious and deceptive objects' (CS 223), in order to thus revalue the boy's natural beauty. The conduct of boys who employed cosmetic assistance, however, was despised as effeminate. An undeceptive virtue in which the being revealed its true beauty was seen as particularly worth striving for. Pleasure should not be intensified by additional attractions – something the lovers of boys accused woman of, who, with her arts of seduction and therefore contrary to nature, attempted to make her husband a slave of pleasure. For the advocates of pederasty, the merely temporary, brief beauty of the boy's body emphasized its uniqueness in comparison with the woman, and justified the virtuousness of his only temporary desirability. Furthermore, in the possible continuation of the relationship between *erastes* and *eromenos* beyond youth they saw the guarantee for the reciprocity of the affective relationship: 'the affection of the one who loves is returned to him by the beloved the way an image is reflected in a mirror' (CS 225).

It was precisely in the arguments listed by the lovers of boys that Foucault saw the emergence of an increasingly converging tendency towards an ethics of marital life. It involved an attempt at reducing obvious differences and beat the lovers of women with their own weapons. The symmetry with which lovers of women threw their weight behind marriage was now to develop from the former asymmetry of the love of boys. Nevertheless in the centre of the controversy there was still a crucial difference between the two ways of life: the Socratic ideal of abstinence whose answer to the question of integration of pleasure was not marriage. Thus the basic premise applied to the *erastes* in the relationship to the boy: 'Remain as chaste as Socrates when he slept beside Alcibiades. Approach them with temperance' (CS 226). The essential point of conflict between marriage and love of boys remained the integration of the pleasures, which tended to hubris and threatened the man's control. It was this fundamental argument of pleasure's integrational capacity which was ultimately to give marriage preference, and allow the ethics of pederasty, in which the problem of the use of pleasures had first been elaborated, to fall into oblivion.

Foucault's 'journey through Greece' came to a close at the point where the theme of love of boys, so central to philosophical tradition in antiquity, was supplanted by a new erotics. On this journey he had acted as an archaeologist in that he brought to light the historical conditions for that process which, via Christianity through to the present day, allowed the exclusivity of heterosexual monogomy. Even before Christianity finally monopolized marriage, 'the temperate love of boys and … its perfection in the lasting form of friendship' (CS 229) soon found its counterpart in an erotics which bore the concern for 'the symmetrical and reciprocal relationship of a man and a woman' (CS 232). From the conflict of using the boy on the one hand as an object of pleasure, and on the other, preserving him from the shame of his degradation, arose the demand for virginity, exceeding Socrates' ascetic ideal. An ethics of pleasure, reserved for the bond between man and wife, grew from that demand for a moderate use of pleasure which originated in the love of boys; this ethics enabled a moderation, linked now to virginity, to develop into the ideal of a perfect union.

Foucault rejected as unsatisfactory, however, traditional attempts to bring the severe ethics of Stoicism into harmony with the inheritance of later Christianity, or to discover parallels for its historical classification. For him this severity was no indication that Christianity would succeed to pagan ethics. According to Foucault, the severity of Stoic ethics could be explained in the attitude towards the sex act, which was considered as dangerous. At the time, this attitude was a care of the self which, in the taming of pleasure, was aiming at an art of existence. Foucault's analysis of the changing sexual ethics of late antiquity, which problematized a greater care for the body's susceptibility and hence the stricter use of its pleasure, was by no means intended to produce analogies to Christianity. On the contrary, he was attempting to show that the demand for self-discipline and strict ethics was inherent in a culture of the self, and should enable one to master one's life. Central to pagan ethics was the fashioning of the self, constituting oneself as moral subject.

Foucault saw marriage as the product of this permanent struggle for one's own sovereignty in self-relation, and the threat to it from daily perils and the challenges of life; the marriage bond should guarantee both partners a higher protection and maintain the order of the more complex social conditions. It is true that the later monopoly of marriage in Christianity can be traced back tendentially to the former's increasing significance in the first two centuries AD, but with regards to an ancient pagan moral reflection, matrimony must be considered in a more sophisticated light than as the solution of an ethical conflict; a conflict which was the result of two possible lifestyles in an epoch of self-care.

For Foucault there was no logical course of historical events and therefore no compelling progression from pagan to Christian ethics. For him the difference lay in the altered form of self-relation: From an ethics of self-concern arose an ethics of self-denial, which also problematized the manner of constituting oneself as moral subject of one's own sexual conduct in a fundamentally different way. It was the 'modalities of the relation to self' which changed; the 'type of work on oneself' (CS 239) which enabled a permanent hermeneutics of desire to develop from a former ethics of existence – a hermeneutics which still obstructs our eyes to that view of ethics Foucault wished to open up. However little a logical principle may be inherent in history, Foucault would have spoken just as little of a 'false development'. It can hardly be denied, however, that with his final studies, Foucault was following Nietzsche's call for the *Umwertung* (revaluation) of an anachronistic tradition bequeathed by Christianity, but still having effect in all areas of modern society, in order to free our view for a culture of the self yet to be created.

Part II:
Foucault's Ethos

'For one thing is needful:
that man should attain contentment with himself.'

(Friedrich Nietzsche, 3/531)

3

The Role of Power

One of the main reasons why Foucault's last studies on an ethics and aesthetics of existence were viewed with so much suspicion and surprise lies in the often asserted thesis that Foucault's primary interest was in the development of an analysis of power phenomena. Foucault himself denied this thesis, and saw his work as a building block in a project which attempted to reconstruct a history of the methods of subjectivization. '[My objective] has not been to analyze the phenomena of power, nor to elaborate the foundations of such an analysis. My objective, instead, has been to create a history of the different modes by which, in our culture, human beings are made subjects' (BSH 208). However, if we want to understand Foucault's alleged change in perspective from an analysis of power to an ethics of existence, as it was executed in his final studies on self-techniques in ancient Greece, it is first necessary to consider more closely the role of power in Foucault's thought, and to clarify whether this is of the central significance implied by his critics again and again.

Although no one seems able to shed any light on the definition of this rather unqualifiable term, there is constantly talk of an apparent 'power theory' which Foucault was supposedly trying to develop. 'Foucault's monistic power theory failed because covertly, it remained the dualistic repression theory of power which it actually wished to overcome.' From this failure, again, the task of Foucault's future research is already inferred, namely 'to draw together these diverging power models into a consistent power theory'.[1] Fink-Eitel's representative focusing of Foucault's studies on the development of a power theory can be understood particularly in view of the latter's project for a six-volume *History of Sexuality*. In an interview in January 1977 – shortly, therefore, after the first volume of the proposed studies on a history of sexuality was published – Foucault expressed himself regarding the motive of his new project as follows: 'The essence of the work for me is a reworking of the theory of power ...' (DE 3/231). A further crucial reason for naming Foucault a theoretician of power can be found in the final chapter of the first volume of *The History of Sexuality*, where he used the term 'bio-power' (HS 140) in the context of the nineteenth century expansion of the capitalist social order. In establishing this order, sexuality was a decisive regulating factor of a bio-power which was to enable the 'controlled insertion of bodies into the machinery of production' and the 'adjustment of the phenomena of population to economic processes' (HS 141).

In this, sexuality not only indicated the whole of life expressions founded in gender but the very phenomenon of regulating 'sex' as a productive factor and, since the eighteenth century (cf. DE 3/313), of installing it as part of a new subjectivization technique. Thus it can be understood why Foucault conceived bio-power as a 'network of somatic-power ... from which sexuality arises as a historical and cultural phenomenon, within which we simultaneously recognize and lose ourselves' (DE 3/231).

Foucault's introduction of the term bio-power, however, is not sufficient to infer a future analysis of power phenomena. Moreover, in the first volume of *The History of Sexuality*, Foucault had already used the power concept in a way which makes its theoretical confinement difficult from the start: 'power is not an institution, and not a structure; neither is it a certain strength we are endowed with; it is the name that one attributes to a complex strategical situation in a particular society' (HS 93).

In fact Foucault did not delve further into the problem of bio-power in modern society, but, as is known, continued his project in another direction. He conceded later, however, that he ought at some point to pursue a 'genealogy of bio-power' (FR 344). Foucault was not interested in the bios' function within the order of the growing production apparatus of modern mass society, but rather in the bios as material for a work of art. This decisive change in his motive cannot be ignored by persistently reproaching Foucault with the failure of his efforts at a power theory. Even if one admits that the problem of power, or rather, the use of power, defined the whole of Foucault's thought, then it was not in the sense of an ambitious project for its theorization, but as an analysis of specific power relations.

Just as Foucault assumed not 'one single fork in reason, but a multiple forking, an unceasing, proliferating bifurcation' (DE 4/440), so he problematized not *one* or *the* power. 'I am therefore no theoretician of power ... Power as a single question does not interest me' (DE 4/451). 'To put it bluntly, I would say that to begin the analysis with a 'how' is to suggest that power as such does not exist'[2] (BSH 217). If Foucault tried to imagine power, then it was as a productive movement, not a repressive one, which, within a diverse and plural web of relations, could change its strategies. For in Foucault's view, 'it is not a question of understanding power as mastery or control, and therefore allowing it to stand as a basic condition, a sole principle of statement or law; rather, power should always be considered as a relationship in a field of interaction, to see it as an indissoluble relation to forms of knowledge, and always to perceive it so it can be seen in a field of possibilities and therefore in a field of reversibility, of possible reverse'[3] (CA 52). 'These relations of power are mobile, reversible and unstable' (DE 4/720).

A metaphysics of power, or a power theory claiming universal validity, would furthermore be absurd for Foucault's investigations, which endeavoured to use science in a way which was not limited to proclaiming theoretical certainties, but which, on the contrary, wanted to make available the means towards a practice of transgressing them. According to Foucault a theory of power would be undesirable and probably also unachievable because the diversity of its lines of strength take form more within a flexible game of ever changing rules than within a theory. For him, what counted was rather the question of how 'the insolubility of knowledge and power in the game of diverse interactions and strategies can lead to singularities, which fix themselves due to their conditions of acceptability, both in a field of possible openings and indecisions, of possible turn-arounds and shifts which make them fragile and impermanent' (CA 52–3).

The challenge in Foucault's thought is underestimated and misunderstood if from the start one questions it as to its possible power-theoretical usefulness – i.e. as to its possible knowledge, its valuable information.[4] Foucault gave no instructions, thus barring himself from a functionalization of his research results. In this respect, the power-theoretical ambitions which some critics accuse him of must be surprising, since they divert Foucault's attention from the actual topic – a history of subjectivization techniques, not power itself. Far from subsuming his works on the subject of madness, the subject of punishment or the subject of desire into a supposedly unified *oeuvre* and postulating the development of a theory of power as the comprehensive aim of the research, the last thing Foucault wanted was this very form of conferring theoretical meaning. He even saw it as incompatible with the ethics of the intellectual, who was not supposed simply to present scientific results, but whose work lay 'in the modification of his own thought, and that of others' (DE 4/675).

Besides, there was nothing Foucault disliked more than a standardization through a theory, a concept or a programme. Instead he was concerned with opportunities for diversification and with showing how power too is of no static or tangible size, but that its potential fragility and vulnerability can be the start of new forms of relationships. The role of power must remain undefined. For Foucault, power was a dynamic process, permanently undergoing development, which resisted being reduced to a 'dualistic repressive hypothesis',[5] appearing rather in temporary forms: in subjects, institutions, discourses. Undertaking the study of complex power relations and bringing their interactions to light means, therefore, studying the gradual formation and establishment of procedures which can be traced back to certain historical conditions; procedures which made man what he appears to be as the contemporary of one or another period of time. But this means neither conjuring up an anthropological ghost nor forcing power into a theoretical straitjacket. Foucault's famous, often quoted words, 'that man would be erased, like a face drawn in sand at the edge of the sea',[6] describe that aspect, characteristic of his thought and undoubtedly linked to Nietzsche, of changeability, transformation, which is inherent in and even conditional for the constitution of human cultural achievements. For man is not an entity 'but only a way, an incident, a bridge' (5/324).

Nothing is evident, nothing must be as it is, nothing stays the same, neither people, nor those instruments of power which allow them to govern and to be governed. Culture is constituted first and foremost as an open, altogether undecided game with changeable, reversible rules and interactions, and 'in such a way that none of these interactions appear to be of priority or absolutely totalizing. Any of them can enter a game which goes beyond them; and conversely, any of them can have an effect, however locally limited it may be, on another to which it belongs and by which it is surrounded. It is then, schematically expressed, a question of a perpetual motion, an intrinsic fragility, of an involvement between process maintenance and process reformation' (CA 52).

For Foucault, then, it was a question of 'strategic analyses' and not a theory of power. Here is also the reason why he did not give a one-sided definition of power as a form of control or domination, as 'evil' or 'repressive'. 'Power is not evil. Power is strategic games' (DE 4/727). This becomes particularly clear in view of Foucault's breaking the spell of the modern idol 'sexuality' as an historically definable figure. Inherent in the promise of a 'sexual revolution' – of being able, through power, to renounce the repression of sex – is the effect, actually produced by this power, of identifying oneself as a sexual being, and hence to desire one's 'sexual liberation'. This was precisely Foucault's meaning when he called sexuality an 'effect with a meaning-value' (HS 176). With this position he emphasized that it was not sufficient for modern liberation movements simply to represent the anti-authoritarian reverse side of the apparently sexually oppressive power, and thus to demand its 'liberation'. Foucault, however, had no way out of this dead end situation to offer in the first volume of *The History of Sexuality*. As is shown by his eight year silence until the publication of the subsequent volumes, he himself was still searching – if not for that solution strategy in the form of a theory of power so often expected of him, then for a feasible way which would lead from the illusion of a liberation to the necessity of an ethical effort at freedom.[7]

Strategic analyses of the games of power, instead of a theory of power, would be the temporary answer regarding the role which Foucault at all conceded to power within the frame of his own definition. Nevertheless, it is questionable whether any role at all can be attributed to power as a theme in Foucault's final studies. In order to explain Foucault's project of a *History of Sexuality* in other terms than as a failure of a power theory, and to comprehend his redirection towards an ethics and aesthetics of existence, the question 'What is power?' should here be replaced by the question 'What is Enlightenment?'

4

The Project of the Genealogies

It was very important to Michel Foucault not to leave the interpretation of his books solely to others. In various essays and interviews Foucault constantly gave his opinion on his books, commenting on them, and where necessary even correcting them; he wrote, under the pseudonym Maurice Florence (cf. DE 4/631–6), a summary of his thought and the most important aims of his studies. This form of intervention, anticipating misunderstandings, nevertheless has another reason, reflecting the consequence of Foucault's plea for a stylistics of existence particularly emphasized in his later work: Such a stylistics of existence namely implies a critical reflection of the contours of his own ethos, of the place of his own thought and tradition. This attempt at a permanent critique of his own thought can be recognized in the whole of Foucault's work, whether in the academic-official function of his 1970 inaugural lecture at the Collège de France;[1] anonymously as the 'philosophe masqué' in an interview ten years later for 'Le Monde' (cf. DE 4/104–10);[2] under a pseudonym in a text written for the 'Dictionnaire des Philosophes'[3] (cf. DE 4/631–6) shortly before his death.

In this last-mentioned Foucault left no doubt as to his thought being part of a philosophical tradition which he expressly connected with the name Kant: '(If Foucault is indeed perfectly at home in the philosophical tradition, it is within the critical tradition of Kant), and his undertaking could be called "A Critical History of Thought"'[4] (DE 4/631). Relating his own thought to a critical questioning of its limits inseparable from Kant is at the same time the key to that philosophical ethos which was at the core of Foucault's final studies on an ethics of self-concern and an aesthetics of existence. With this Foucault was trying to do justice to his own claim of pursuing a critical ontology of the self, and defining this as still the primary task of the Enlightenment. To this extent Foucault did not problematize his relationship to Kant here, but first emphasized Kant's merit for having answered the question 'What is Enlightenment?' – decisive for modern philosophy – with a critical-reflexive attitude towards his own thought and present-day relevance. The exposition which followed is therefore not so much dedicated to Kant's work as to Foucault's own role as enlightener and critic. For Foucault this role of criticism was concentrated in the question of what we are today. It essentially comprehends two aspects: A genealogy which attempts to diagnose the present in a critical questioning of origin, and an ontology of that which, due to this origin, made us what we are today.

GENEALOGY AS DIAGNOSIS OF THE PRESENT

For Foucault, *Aufklärung* (Enlightenment) was not a particular, faded episode in the history of philosophy, but was in essence characterized by that feature with which 'philosophical thought had sought to reflect on its own present' (FR 33) and to ask about the 'contemporary reality' (FR 34). 'We must pose ourselves the question: what is today?' (DE 4/448) 'What is happening at the present, and what are we who are perhaps nothing other than that which is currently happening? The question of philosophy is the question about this present, which we ourselves are' (DE 3/266).

To pose the question about the present means at the same time to reconstruct its origin from the past, and to write its history. Only the technical equipment appearing in the wings relativizes the view of the actual events on the stage, and helps to understand the contexts of the effects. For behind Foucault's historical studies – whether on the Greek antiquity or the history of madness between the sixteenth and eighteenth centuries – there is no nostalgia or 'backward-looking Utopia',[5] but precisely the attempt to create a 'positive relation' (TS 12) to one's own present. This relationship is not limited to considering the present as progress with regards to the past, nor to portraying it as 'better, or more developed or more enlightened' (DE 2/750).

Foucault's understanding of history is of key significance with respect to his accentuation of the present and his desire for a transformation of current ways of thought. He is not a historian in the classical sense of a chronicler or preserver of past epochs, but in the express context of wishing to pursue a critical analysis of the

present. A disinterested study of history for its own sake was just as
foreign to Foucault as the backward-looking lingering in the
museum-like arsenal of times past. Foucault pleaded instead for a
contemporary use of history, neither illuminated by the glory beam
of golden eras, nor darkened with the shadows of barbaric epochs,
but one which throws light on the here and now.

Furthermore, he did not view history as the progress of human
culture from its origin to the promise of its completion. For
Foucault, history was a process which, like life itself, is essentially
inconsistent, contingent, open and fragile, thus in Nietzsche's
sense a 'plastic power' (1/251) rather than a continuum. More
important than the historical study itself was the 'archaeological
description, and its concern to establish thresholds, ruptures, and
transformations', in order then to confront them 'with the true
work of historians, which is to reveal continuities' (AK 204).
'History is a vague terrain, not a firing range', comparable to an
'upheaval in the kaleidoscope, not a continuation of growth',[6] as
Paul Veyne writes, who praises Foucault as a perfected historian.[7]
This over-hasty professional categorization, however, could hardly
have been in Foucault's interest, whose interdisciplinary method of
working can also be interpreted as an attempt to avoid being ruled
by occupational status. It is true that Foucault once admitted to
being a 'happy positivist' (AK 125), but this emphasis related to a
methodological quality, not to a professional guild. In this sense,
Deleuze's switch to more descriptive categories like those of the
'new archivist'[8] is to be preferred. Foucault himself, well known for
his aversion to allocations of identity, avoided academic role distribution: 'I am a dealer in tools, an issuer of prescriptions, a sign post,
a cartographer, a drawer of plans, a weapon smith' (DE 2/725). The
heterogenities in the many-faceted kaleidoscope of history which
came under Foucault's inspection are, moreover, foreign to a coher-
ent, meaningful writing of history. Instead of assuming a teleology
of the historical process, Foucault's analyses serve rather an indi-
vidualizing within the suspenseful game of the 'sub-historical'
connections of function and effect. Where others believe they are
seeing or giving sense, Foucault saw the sober process of a functioning without myths. 'There is, indeed, no point to humanity. It
functions, controls its functioning, and constantly gives justification for this control. We have to accept that they are only
justifications' (DE 1/619).

Desmond Bell also made it clear that, with regard to the

problematic difference and relationship between the present and history, it was important for Foucault to prove, by a critical genealogy of present-day problems, the absurdity of the very myths of progress and telos of history.[9] Instead of this 'the return to history finds its sense in the extent to which history shows that that which is, has not always been. It joins chance meetings into the thread of a fragile and uncertain history ... which we can completely construct and regain from the web of contingencies' (DE 4/449). From this Foucault did not conclude that history determines mankind's present, but that it is in itself similar to a force field, whose contingent constellations lead, under certain conditions, to ascertainable cultural phenomena. Foucault's historical studies attempted to show that the present does not have to be simply the result of a compulsory historical necessity, but that, in experiencing its limits, we have the opportunity to take an active part in life's formation. The present is the result of 'innumerable and very concrete human practices, and as such, can be changed by other practices'.[10]

With the analysis of current problems through the revelation of their historical constitution, Foucault drew attention to this very potential of changeability. At this point, in view of the later definition of an aesthetics of existence, it could be anticipated that the possibility for transformation inherent in every process was the decisive aspect for Foucault. For it does not lead to the dead end of sense-giving or a forced meaning, but to an aesthetical interpretation of the world through the fashioning of one's self. Foucault's questions to history, then, served precisely to allow us to reemerge from it – in favour of an altered outlook on current problems and how to overcome them, how to overcome ourselves. His retrospective look at history was an aesthetical view, a revising or recreating which hardly corresponded to the goals of conventional history. The question of Enlightenment is in this sense to be seen as an appeal to grasp the present as a feature of possibility, as a lifelong challenge to fashion that which is to come. In this, history did not serve Foucault as a factual study, but as a revelation of the possibilities for a cultural transformation which reached into the future: Foucault's interest in history was aesthetically motivated.

If Foucault's central question was 'What are we now?', then it remains to be answered where he himself took his place in the interplay between the analysis of the present and the concentrated historical studies for this analysis. Clare O'Farrell took this question as the theme for her book: *Foucault: Historian or Philosopher?*[11] Her answer reads like a Foucauldian evasion manoeuvre, although less subtle: 'Foucault is a philosopher who writes history, transforming it into philosophy.'[12] The unsatisfying nature of this response reflects all the more clearly the effort to fix Foucault's thought, and make it tangible. Foucault had his own answer to O'Farrell's question – one which consciously shied clear of any commitment: 'If philosophy is memory or a return of the origin, what I am doing cannot, in any way, be regarded as philosophy; and if the history of thought consists in giving life to half-effaced figures, what I am doing is not history either' (AK 206). In *The Archaeology of Knowledge*, Foucault had in fact tried to distance himself from conventional methods and goals, both as historian and philosopher, and attempted to make use of science in a manner originating in the thought of Nietzsche, who tore 'the thread of transcendental teleologies' (AK 131), and liberated 'the history of thought from its subjection to transcendence' (AK 203). In this respect it is doubtful whether the alternatives 'history or philosophy' has any sense at all for Foucault's work.

We should not succumb to the compulsion to categorize Foucault's research as historical or philosophical, but should return to the standpoint from which Foucault posed his questions: The present day.[13] Foucault expressed his kind of studies very clearly: 'I start with a problem as it is currently posed, and try to produce its genealogy. Genealogy means that I conduct the analysis from a present-day question' (DE 4/674). According to this definition, genealogy is a method of contributing to the explanation of how present-day cultural phenomena arose, through their historical derivation and constitution.[14] To this extent, Foucault can be termed a genealogist. Genealogy forms the bridge to that present which concerned Foucault not merely for reasons of contemporariness. To live in one's time, in the here and now, implied for Foucault the ethical endeavour to gain a critical relation to the culture and forces which constitute one's own being. Only our own distancing enlightenment and maturity allow the genealogies to become 'anti-sciences' (DE 3/165), from which we proceed as a different person to that which we were before. For genealogical knowledge must be applicable in 'present-day tactics' and 'must fight against the very power effects of a discourse seen as scientific' (DE 3/166).

Genealogy is an 'anti-science' in the sense that it is the attempt to problematize the present time. It does not produce truths and certainties, but is a strategy of resistance. The results of genealogy do not, therefore, confer identity, nor serve a 'uniform theory' (DE 3/165) but are disturbing and should awaken us to the very dangers of scientific monopolization. The present's historical context, made visible by genealogy, i.e. the development of the present from the material of the past, should contribute to the recognition that nothing is evident or obvious – and therefore does not have to be. That was the political, fighting side of Foucault's genealogical undertaking. 'Genealogy reveals the contingency, even arbitrariness, of our apparently natural and necessary understanding of ourselves.'[15]

Central to genealogy, in its gearing to the present and as a critical ontology of ourselves, is a function which can be traced back to Nietzsche:[16] It delivers the diagnostic apparatus of philosophy. For, since Nietzsche, the task of philosophy is no longer confined to finding a truth 'which is valid for all times. I am just trying to diagnose: to *diagnose the present*. I am trying to say what we are today, and what it now means to say the things we say' (DE 1/606). In this emphatic context of philosophy as a diagnosis of the present, Foucault saw himself as a philosopher, and not in the Platonic sense of a proclaimer of universal truths. Here genealogy forms the interface between an archaeological coming-to-terms with history, and a critical, diagnostic philosophy. 'Genealogy focuses on "the moment of arising" not "as the final term of an historical development" but as a diagnosis.'[17]

GENEALOGY AS AN HISTORICAL ONTOLOGY

Along with this general definition of genealogy as a diagnosis and problematization of the present, it remains to be clarified which specific present Foucault was questioning in his final books.[18] The question about the present peaks in the question about the 'we': '… the subject … is the general theme of my research' (BSH 209). 'I have dealt with the modern theoretical constitutions that were concerned with the subject in general.'[19] In this a genealogy of the subject is outlined by three central questions: 'How are we constituted as subjects of our own knowledge? How are we constituted as subjects who exercise or submit to power relations? How are we constituted as the moral subjects of our own actions?' (FR 49).

Foucault's primary concern was the subject and not, therefore, the constituting of power.

If the subject is accepted as the general theme for Foucault's research, the following perspectives for his work arise: In *The Order of Things* he posed the problem of the subject in its theoretical definition as a speaking, living and working being within scientific discourse. In a more practice-orientated manner, the subject concerned Foucault with regards to his institutional shaping in the sphere of influence of hospitals, asylums and prisons, where certain subjects (the sick, the mad, the delinquent) were made into objects of both knowledge and control (*The Birth of the Clinic, Madness and Civilization, Discipline and Punish*).

The fact that Foucault was accused of a theory of power may further have an understandable reason in that these forms of subjectivization were essentially directed at types of control and domination, i.e. they concerned the processes 'by which, in our culture, human beings are made subjects' (BSH 208). However, the appearance of the first volume of *The History of Sexuality* announced a change which was to become perfectly apparent eight years later, with the publication of his last two books: Using the example of the modern experience of sexuality, Foucault left the 'passive', 'negative' level of domination-forms behind him, and turned to those 'active', 'positive' forms of understanding which the subject creates about himself. Foucault's interest shifted from the coercion of the subjectivization processes to the practice of self-formation of the subject, his 'autoformation' (DE 4/709). This qualitative change in his research is revealed in the first volume of *The History of Sexuality* through the rejection of the so-called 'repressive hypothesis': Instead of dwelling on a repressive power which taboos sex, Foucault wanted to analyse the very 'inciting power' (DE 3/106) which persistently produces sex, and therefore actually gives reason for 'sexuality'. Foucault still held on to the thought of offering 'simultaneously the draft for an analysis of power, through a fragmentary history of the 'science of sex' (DE 3/106). Thus the revelation of this productive reverse side of power was not understood by his critics as the relationship between the subject and those effects of power and truth manifested in sexuality; a relationship difficult for Foucault himself, and which was not to be reduced simply to the level of repression. The critics saw it as nothing but a dead end route to theoretical entanglements with power.[20]

Foucault's realization that he was concentrating mainly on the problem of the subject, or rather, 'reintroducing the problem of the subject' (DE 4/705), came later, and was due to his studies on sexuality. Instead of the five further volumes originally planned, which were to follow the first volume with a detailed history of sexuality and which were intended to deal with themes such as the sexualization of the child, the specification of the pervert, and the hystericalization of the woman, Foucault decided in favour of an 'about-turn' (cf. DE 4/670). In his early work, *Histoire de la Folie*,[21] he had already used the example of madness to study the process of its 'social, political and epistemological' (DE 4/670) 'imprisonment', thus exposing the 'other', hidden face of reason and its chattering silence.

In the same way, with a history of sexuality, Foucault wanted to try to describe the subject of the pervert or the child as part of a 'sexual imprisonment'.[22] For this reason, Foucault was also seen as a 'thinker of imprisonment, of subjugated, constrained and disciplined subjects' (DE 4/675), as one who produced evidence for the extremely foreign reality of institutional, yet scientific detention.[23] 'The man described for us, whom we are invited to free, is already in himself the effect of a subjection much more profound than himself.'[24] After the publication of the first volume of *The History of Sexuality* in 1976, Foucault abandoned this problematization of subjugation modes, i.e. the manner in which the historically developed forms of rule function as types of government and subjugation, and the analysis of bodies 'which are constituted as subjects by the effects of power' (DE 3/180). 'It is now about the manner in which we govern ourselves' (DE 4/670). Although this profound change from the process of subjectivization to the question of self-constitution maintains the general theme of the subject, the manner of problematization has become another, more affirmative one.

In order to understand this decisive turning point in Foucault's later work, it is necessary to recall the point of origin of his studies on sexuality, to see what qualitative alteration the general theme of the subject has undergone. Foucault's motive for a history of sexuality was to reconstruct genealogically the hermeneutic subject of desire, and to show why today we reveal ourselves as desiring subjects, or, more precisely, why we have made a moral experience out of sexuality. 'Finally, I have sought to study ... the way *a human being turns him- or herself into a subject* ... how men have learned to recognize themselves as subjects of "sexuality"' (BSH 208) (my italics).

But Foucault's genealogy of the subject of desire should not be seen merely as a critical attitude towards the predominant modern 'sexual ethics' and their homage to the 'sex idol'; it is also directed in particular against the activity sphere of psychoanalysis. It was in precisely this context that Foucault attempted to write the history of sexuality as an 'archaeology of psychoanalysis' (HS 130). Archaeology here means the attempt to reveal the epistemological layers which have led to today's deployment of sexuality, thus bringing to light those historical conditions from which psycho-analysis could be constituted as a hermeneutics of desire. For Foucault, the roots of the psychoanalytical subject of desire lay in Christian morality; the hermeneutic subject was the result of proce-dures of confession originating in the Christian confessional. Considered in this light, Foucault's final studies on an aesthetics of existence should be seen as a 'counter-draft' to psychoanalysis, that is, as an attempt, not to get behind the truth of desire, but to view pleasures as innate impulses natural to everybody, to be integrated moderately in a stylistics of existence. This becomes particularly clear in the introductory chapter of *The Care of the Self* about Artemidorus' *The Interpretation of Dreams*, which can be read as a differentiation between the ancient dream criticism of Artemidor and the modern dream interpretation of Freud.[25]

But Foucault was not content to trace back genealogically the subject of desire in the psychoanalytical confessional to its histori-cal beginnings in Christianity; nor to acknowledge the demand of the so-called liberation movements to achieve the subject's emanci-pation by the deceptive promise of a sexual revolution. In his effort to find a way out of the dilemma of modern sexual morality, Foucault went far back to the beginnings of Western moral history: to ancient techniques of the self, as yet undimmed by a morphol-ogy of desire. Here the problem was not yet a hermeneutic searching for the truth of desire, but the study of 'the games of truth in the relationship of self with self and the forming of oneself as a subject' (UP 6).

This decisive and incisive alteration in his project led Foucault also to the late recognition that his fundamental theme was the subject, and not the analysis of power. But this also led to an exten-sion of the question of what we are today. Basically, this lies in a new perspective which Foucault opened up with regard to the subject. With similar reasons to those with which he rejected the power-concept and the possibility of a theory of power, Foucault executed the dismantling of the term 'subject'. While before it was still a question of the historical constitution of the various subject forms (e.g. the 'mad' and the 'normal' subject) in relation to the games of truth or the wielding of power, Foucault now, in his analysis of pagan self-techniques, turned to the manner in which 'the subject constitutes himself in an active fashion, by the practices of the self' (DE 4/719). We are by no means to conclude from this that Foucault had been aiming for a 'theory of the subject' in his previous studies.[26] In his earlier studies as well he had intended quite the opposite, and had tried to show that neither the subject, nor power and truth are something given, but rather are the matter for something transformable. All his works can be interpreted as the attempt to give the lie to the supposed unity of the subject by persistently revealing the various processes by which people become 'subjects'. 'I have tried to get out from the philosophy of the subject through a genealogy of this subject, by studying the constitution of the subject across history which has led us up to the modern concept of the self.'[27]

In this respect Foucault rejected a concept of the subject which suggested the latter's substantial unity, and which took no account of the complexity of the subjectivization processes. This becomes clear in his studies of pagan self-technologies; these no longer approach the subject from the side of his subjugation, but from the side of his sovereignty, i.e. a person's ethical concern. It is this 'about-turn' from the subjugated subject to the sovereign, responsible moral subject of oneself in the ancient world which allowed Foucault to reject emphatically the concept of a given authentic self – a concept which all his genealogical works were meant to shatter. '... I would simply say that there is no subject' (DE 4/706). For Foucault, therefore, the ancient Greek experience of a moral problematization of pleasures within an ethical framework of a necessary, as yet undeveloped self-constitution, betrays most clearly the modern illusion that one has only to 'free' oneself of imposed norms (sexual, social etc.). The aim of this genealogy of the modern subject of desire, reaching back to antiquity, namely to Plato, was then an ontology of ourselves which did not try – like Sigmund Freud or, more vehemently, Wilhelm Reich – to emancipate and liberate the authentic self from the burden of repression, but which rejected its allocated identity in favour of an invention of the self and a stylistics of existence.

GENEALOGY AS A TRANSFORMATIVE EXPERIMENT

Together with the two time levels of genealogy previously indicated under the general theme of the subject – present and past – another time axis in the process of development appears: the future. This nourishes Foucault's desire to consider genealogy as an experiment, to go beyond given limits and to create new forms of subjectivity. In his historical analyses, from *Histoire de la Folie* to the first volume of a *Histoire de la Sexualité*, Foucault had undertaken a critique of the present and of ourselves through the genealogies of the subject of madness, delinquency and desire. The results were not supposed to help abandon the future to a contingent course of events, but should be useful as an instrument of resistance, as 'tool boxes' (DE 2/720) or even as 'molotov cocktails' (DE 2/725) for those who wish to reject identification with the status quo – this with reference not only to the status quo of power.

Foucault's project of the genealogies would indeed have had the 'nihilistic impact'[28] which Desmond Bell accused it of, if it were to be understood as an insistence on the mere development of the subject. But Foucault's glance did not dwell on the inescapable nature of a subject's historical constitution, but rather was directed at the future of his potential transformation. Foucault's genealogy of the subject was experimental in so far as it attempted to guess, in the sense of Nietzsche, the conditions 'under which future people live – because such a guess and anticipation has the *power* of a motive: The future, as that which we want it to be, affects our Now' (10/237). Genealogy, then, is a critique of the present, in that it considers it desirable to transgress the limits of the present, and encourages us, through the ontology of ourselves, to face the challenge of new tasks.

Foucault's genealogy, directed at the future, did not prophesy or promise, but was founded on present-day problems in the here and now, and the possibilities for their change. The future for him was an open horizon and dispensed with any ultimate purpose; it embodied no faith in progress, promised no humanistic ideals, and spurned the religious comfort of reincarnation. Foucault's programmeless future contained, at best, hopes 'of a new age of curiosity' (DE 4/108). The future was the yet to be fashioned freedom, the challenge, reaching into the present, to make of one's life a work worthy of recollection for future generations. For Foucault, the future was an open-ended game, in which – in

Nietzsche's self-affirmative sense – 'one becomes what one is' (6/293). This stipulates, however, that one has no ready-made ideal of oneself, but rather, through looking with 'more eyes, different eyes' (5/365), one attains a perspective and genealogical view of things.

The most important consequence which Foucault inferred from his finding that there is no authentic subject – and that therefore the subject does not exist as something intrinsic – was an ontology of the self with the future-orientated aim of becoming a different person to that which one is, or has been up to now. 'From the idea that the self is not given to us, I think that there is only one practical consequence: we have to create ourselves as a work of art' (FR 351). Foucault intentionally left open the question as to the appearance of such an artwork of the self, or how a future culture, based on an aesthetics of existence, should be created.[29] Instead he encouraged us not simply to identify with the existing culture, but to understand culture as something which first has to be created. 'We have to realize cultural creations … I don't know what we would do to form these creations, and I don't know what forms these creations would take.'[30] For Foucault, mankind had no hidden purpose which had to be discovered; there is no abyss lying in the dark depths of being which betrays to us what we truly are. Man is something developing, unfinished, which is more a reason for a creative activity than for a hermeneutic decipherment. Considered thus, Foucault was not making a normative use of ethics, but an inventive one, to 'constitute oneself as the worker on the beauty of one's own life' (DE 4/671).

Foucault's genealogy encouraged the experiment of transformation, and with this an ontological position from which a person, as the artist of his own life, is continuously starting over and questioning his limits. In this sense, Foucault's genealogical project as a question of an attitude to life, is 'timeless' and ahistorical; it is closest to Nietzsche's idea of recurrence, which detaches itself from epochal classifications, asking not about the 'typical modern era' but about modernity as an attitude to life.

5

Modernity as an Attitude

Foucault insisted that the question 'What is Enlightenment?' had still not lost anything of its significance for modern philosophy after Kant's essay was published in the *Berlinische Monatsschrift* (*Berlin Monthly*) in 1784. This is seen in Foucault's own attempt,[1] which should be mentioned here, to approach the question of the Enlightenment ethically and politically, namely as a question of attitude, connecting this with the courage of the individual and not looking on it as a critique serving the 'great process of rendering society governable' (CA 40). Foucault saw this critique as forming three areas: the positivist science, the constitution of the modern state and the political science which to a certain extent linked these two. Instead of delving further into the problem of rendering modern society governable in these areas, and into that of the state 'bio-politics' (HS 139) – as might have been expected after the first volume of *The History of Sexuality* – Foucault paid increased attention to the critical attitude inherent in the question of the Enlightenment, which gave precedence to the ethical problem of individual conduct and government over that of the collective. Foucault tried to make apparent that critical attitude connected with the Enlightenment, before it 'slipped over' into a project on criticism. 'Could we not try to take this road again – but in the other direction? And if we have to raise the question of knowledge and its relation to domination, this would be due first and foremost to a decisive will not to be governed, the decisive will – an attitude both individual and at the same time collective – to get out, as Kant says, of one's immaturity. *A question of attitude*' (CA 53) (my italics).

For Foucault, therefore, of interest in Kant's essay was 'that the "way out" that characterizes Enlightenment is a process that releases us from the status of "immaturity"' (FR 34). For Foucault, Kant's heraldic device 'Sapere aude' – 'dare to know', 'have the courage, the audacity, to know' (FR 35) – was connected to the individual's courage to act from the here and now, and to test his independence in the reflexive, critical use of his reason, and in a daily 'act of courage' (FR 35). The question of attitude was also more important here for Foucault than the question about an ethical universal rule. Enlightenment begins with the individual's commitment 'as an act of courage to be accomplished personally' (FR 35) and which is prerequisite for 'the constitution of the self as an autonomous subject' (FR 42). But the critical, in other words, the neither dogmatic nor unlimited use of reason should be seen as a condition for the Enlightenment. This critical use is 'the business of the subject himself as an individual' and 'must not be conceived simply as a general process affecting all humanity' (FR 37). For Foucault, the Enlightenment took its starting point in the constitu-tion of the sovereign, mature moral subject in self-relation, and not in any purpose relating to humanity as a whole. For 'sovereign moral subject of oneself' means the use of reason as a moral problem for managing one's conduct. Here the word 'moral' should be replaced with 'critical', and 'subject' with 'individual'. For, analogous to genealogy as a critique of the present, Foucault now, with the question of the Enlightenment as one of the critical attitudes of the individual, returned to the genealogical 'substra-tum' of a 'subject' who is no longer in servitude to history, but who cares for himself in the light of his specific present.

This critical reflection of the present as an ontology of the self-striving for maturity was both a 'permanent critique of our historical era' (FR 42) and, for Foucault, the essential element of what he called the attitude of modernity, and which he conceived as the fundamental motive of modern philosophy. However little he interpreted Enlightenment exclusively in the context of Kant's work, and instead was interested from the start in 'the philosophi-cal question of the present day' (FR 34) in Kant's Enlightenment essay, as little did Foucault reduce the concept of modernity to the specificity of an epoch. For him, the attribute 'modern ' was not 'situated on a calendar' in which 'it would be preceded by a more or less naive or archaic premodernity, and followed by an enig-matic and troubling "postmodernity"' (FR 39).[2] Foucault did not see the so-called modern age as simply a temporary period of time which could later be classified historically and therefore become reducible in terms of time; rather it was an attitude designated as 'a mode of relating to contemporary reality; a voluntary choice made by certain people; ... a way, too, of acting and behaving that at one and the same time marks a relation of belonging and presents itself as a task' (FR 39). But if the attitude of modernity cannot be fixed historically, it is not just a characteristic of an epoch appearing with the Enlightenment; rather modernity should be understood as a style of existence which is present in the whole cultural history of mankind, a form which reached particular peaks from antiquity through the Renaissance to the 'postmodern' labelling of the present.[3] Christianity and its variety of influences, including a hermeneutics of the subject, which essentially dominated the over 2,000-year interim of Western history, belonged to those attitudes which Foucault termed 'countermodernity' (FR 39). Thus, from the Kantian Enlightenment to the Greek ethos, the motive of Foucault's final studies emerges as a genealogical critique of the counter-modern. However, instead of simply comparing the attitude of the modern era with Greek ethos and demonstrating their affinity, in his response to the Enlightenment question Foucault drew near to his own present, selecting a personality more closely related to his own life and work than Kant: Charles Baudelaire.

For Foucault, Baudelaire personified the artist's will 'to "heroize" the present' (FR 40); that is, to counter the fleeting, contingent, temporary movement of the present with the gravity of one's own being, and not simply to sink in the quicksand of mere existence. The present is that ever-escaping moment in which the contingency and freedom of being is experienced most urgently. It allows people to catch that brief glimpse of the movement of life itself, and to sense that nothing remains as it was. For Baudelaire, this unique, transformative movement of the present did not hide the mystery of time, but rather challenged him to take a stance towards life. This lay not simply in the approval of the immediate reality, but in the challenge to participate in the fleeting process of development, and to integrate into one's own life the permanent movement of change, the desire for transformation which is inherent to life. Between Baudelaire and the present there existed 'a difficult inter-play between the truth of what is real and the exercise of freedom' (FR 41).

This will for transformation described as a game between truth and freedom, characterizes not only Baudelaire's attitude to modernity, but Foucault's own ethos too. It is in this context that we should understand his comment that he 'never wrote anything other than fictions' (DE 3/236). For the motive of his genealogies was not simply to clarify the development of the truth, but to take this knowledge of present reality as a starting point of a work on the yet-to-be-fashioned freedom of one's life, and to imagine the present 'otherwise than it is, and to transform it not by destroying it but by grasping it in what it is. Baudelairean modernity is an exercise in which extreme attention to what is real is confronted with the practice of a liberty that simultaneously respects this reality and violates it' (FR 41). If fiction denotes the interplay between truth and the possibility to replace truth with something different, something new, then Foucault's books are fictitious in the sense that they express the will to know as the will to be different, and do not simply remain within the present domain of truth.[4]

This point of view seems to resemble more the creative activity of the artist Baudelaire rather than that truth-entrusted work of the philosopher Foucault. But this difference exists above all due to the conception that art and philosophy are two different areas of human culture which, at best, complement each other. Foucault wished however to diminish this discrepancy with his targeted philosophical ethos as an attitude of modernity. He tried to distance himself from a conception of art 'which is related only to objects and not to individuals, or to life' (FR 350) – a conception, therefore, which remains limited to the relationship between artist and artwork; further, he attempted 'to use philosophy in a way that would permit' him 'to limit the domains of knowledge' (DE 4/707). Similarly to the demand to create one's life, i.e. ourself as a work of art, one should choose, 'among all the things that you can know through scientific knowledge only those kinds of things which were relative to him and important to life' (FR 360).[5]

Modernity as an attitude not only problematizes the critical relationship to one's own present, but further attempts to integrate art and philosophy as a living practice of an aesthetics and ethics of existence, i.e. in an individual, singular life design. Thus it is no longer the sculpture created by the artist, nor the philosopher's academic work on moral norms and maxims, but the individual himself as a creator of his own lifework. Aesthetics and ethics of existence then, is not confined to a visit to an art exhibition, nor is it 'necessary to relate ethical problems to scientific knowledge' (FR 349).

This aesthetical and ethical stance of modernity, which cannot be separated from one's own existence, and which presupposes a relationship to oneself, was termed by Baudelaire 'dandyism'. 'The deliberate attitude of modernity is tied to an indispensable asceticism' requiring that one takes 'oneself as object of a complex and difficult elaboration' (FR 41). Foucault, however, did not view asceticism in the Christian sense of abstinence, but in antiquity's sense of 'the work one performs on oneself, in order to transform oneself or to allow that self to appear, which one luckily never achieves' (DE 4/165). In precisely this manner, Baudelaire embodied for Foucault 'the asceticism of the dandy who makes of his body, his behavior, his feelings and passions, his very existence, a work of art' (FR 41–2). Instead of putting his trust in psychoanalytical or even esoteric practices of a supposed 'self-finding' or 'liberating', so as to thus discover his 'authentic', suppressed self, Baudelaire's modern dandy is a person in need of fundamental shaping, who 'tries to invent himself' and who faces up to 'the task of producing himself' (FR 42).

Fictions, change, transformation, otherness, invention – all concepts are not merely an expression for a simple travesty or an ironical breaking of reality, but stand for the will to fashion a work of art by working as a strict and critical stylist of one's own lifework. But the nineteenth century dandy is not the only representative of this stylistics of existence;[6] also Foucault's lifework itself is one, less as an academic undertaking than as an attempt at aesthetical experience. This perspective on his work brought on the repeated accusation that Foucault was avoiding a clear scientific position.[7] Yet it is precisely to Foucault's credit that he showed through his work that knowledge alone does not suffice to change the world or one's own life; that what is important is to develop an attitude, a philosophical ethos. For Foucault, scientific work was not limited to an explanation of our development, but was based on the conviction that we should take an active and transforming role in fashioning the process of development through the example of our own existence. In this sense, Foucault was not an academic; his historical research was fictional and experimental, transforming the present, in as far as it already contained the seed of that which could be thought. '[I]t's true that I am not a really good academic. For my intellectual work is related to what you could call aestheticism, meaning transforming yourself. I believe my problem is this strange relationship between knowledge, scholarship, theory and real history ... I am not interested in the academic status of what I am doing because my problem is my own transformation ... This transformation of one's self by one's own knowledge is I think something rather close to the aesthetic experience.'[8] 'I am an experimenter and not a theoretician' (DE 4/42). With this stance, which he termed 'aesthetical experience', towards his own work, Foucault wanted to point out that his studies, like other scientific discourses, also produce certain truth-effects. Nevertheless, Foucault did not require 'truthfulness' or 'authenticity' of his historical analyses, but 'beauty' – not as a thing of taste, but as the art of transforming one's own thought. In this sense – as will be shown later – Foucault was absolutely Nietzschean, and his project was the attempt to integrate the aesthetic attitude into science, to open doors to a 'gay science'.

A permanent criticism and a creation of ourselves are the bases for an aesthetics and ethics of existence which are described by Foucault through the examples of both Baudelaire and ancient Greece, and which together form the problem of modern philosophy. In this a critical use of one's reason in constituting self-knowledge is prerequisite for a transformation of the self. This 'self-invention' of the individual is based neither on an ethical theory nor on an aesthetical doctrine, but is viewed, according to modernity, as an attitude, a style of existence. For this reason the resistance towards the many ghosts of humanism, including Habermas's firm belief in the remedy of communication,[9] which is apparent throughout Foucault's *oeuvre*, is understandable: through its promises, humanism holds people back from a critical, creative work on themselves, basically serving 'to color and to justify the conceptions of man' (FR 44). Both Christianity and that humanism which gives central place to the entity 'man', were seen by Foucault as examples of countermodernity to be faced with mistrust and scepticism. The image of mankind praised behind the mask of humanism should give way to the attempt at a transforming exercise of oneself, thus smoothing the way for a person fighting on the border between supposed necessity and as yet unformed freedom.

For this reason Foucault saw a criticism which rejected humanism as consisting precisely in the analysis of limits and their reflection. Between the reality of the given, the necessary, and the freedom of the arbitrary and contingent, man stands as a changing and creating force. Foucault named this unique position of man 'limit-attitude' (FR 45).[10] Here he was concerned with transforming the theoretical critique of the existing, apparently necessary reality, intended as an historical study, 'into a practical critique that takes the form of a possible transgression' (FR 45). Criticism then, for Foucault, was expressly not intended to search for 'formal structures with universal value' (FR 46), but rather to make comprehensible how we have constituted ourselves, and are prepared to acknowledge ourselves, as subjects of action and knowledge. Foucault's critique as limit-attitude was levelled against a transcendental concept of experience, and against any form of metaphysical promise. Instead he made a plea for an archaeology revealing historical layers in *this* world, and for a genealogy which in this way diagnoses the present; a genealogy which, 'from the contingency that has made us what we are', allows us to find 'the possibility of no longer being, doing, or thinking what we are, do, or think' and through which we can try 'to give new impetus, as far and wide as possible, to the undefined work of freedom' (FR 46).

With his books as an expression of an experimental limit-attitude, and as a work of freedom, Foucault was attempting to navigate between the Scylla of universal necessity and the Charybdis of arbitrariness, thus revealing the game of true or false as a changeable, and therefore reversible, relationship of powers. In so doing, Foucault showed that freedom is not a universal good. It is a critical work, to be performed on oneself, necessary in order to escape the dangers of dependence and subjugation. According to this, the concept of freedom is defined not simply as being free of constraints, but as an ethical strategy of a 'de-subjugation' (CA 39) which demands lifelong vigilance from him who wishes to retain control of himself. In this it is not enough merely to free oneself of unpleasantness; one must recognize the dangers which threaten the work of freedom. The strategy of de-subjugation puts before us the daily 'ethico-political choice ... to determine which is the main danger'. 'If everything is dangerous, then we always have something to do' (FR 343).

Foucault also termed the work of freedom as 'a hyper- and pessimistic activism' (FR 343) which demands a diagnostic of dangers through the exact study of current problems. In this sense, freedom is 'the ontological condition of ethics' (DE 4/712), and Enlightenment a philosophical attitude, which is crucial 'where change is possible and desirable' (FR 46). This referred not only to Foucault's own works on the practices of psychiatry or punishment, and the desirability of reforming them, but also to the technologies of the self for protection against the latent danger of a hubris of pleasures. Such an attitude requires flexibility and a vital readiness for change. For this reason, the Enlightenment as a critical ontology of ourselves should not be considered 'as a theory, a doctrine, nor even as a permanent body of knowledge that is accumulating; it has to be conceived as an attitude, an ethos, a philosophical life in which the critique of what we are is at one and the same time the historical analysis of the limits that are imposed on us and an experiment with the possibility of going beyond them' (FR 50). The question of the Enlightenment was for Foucault, then, essentially a question of attitude, which attempts at each point in history and in life – whether in the time of Socrates or of Baudelaire, in youth or in old age – to fathom the historical constitutional conditions of the here and now. Recognizing this contingency of being, however, should not lead to an apathetic attitude to one's helplessness, but to the subsequent option of making one's life a work of art. Foucault's works do not then, demonstrate the viewpoint popular with some nihilists, 'that the system has swallowed us all'; rather, through a critique of this system – or more precisely, these systems – they smooth the way towards greater maturity and resistance, in order to transform that order of things which we had been made to believe was self-evident and irrevocable.

6

The Care of the Truth

The entire critical-occidental tradition of philosophical questioning can be understood as an epistemological project of an analysis of truth, an 'obligation of truth' (DE 4/723). This concern for the truth reads from Plato to Hegel like the history of an obsession, in which attempts to undermine this tradition remain marginal. 'Things being as they are, nothing so far has shown that it is possible to define a strategy outside of this concern' (DE 4/723–4). With Nietzsche a counter-movement became powerful enough to prepare the ground for a 'different thought' through the genealogy of the will for truth prevalent until then. Seen in this light, Nietzsche's philosophy is the life-story of a struggle against the Platonic monopoly of truth. In this context Nietzsche saw Christian monotheism as the greatest expression of the call for truthfulness, simply because it was embodied in one God. For Nietzsche, the term 'God' was the 'counterconcept of life' par excellence (6/373). His diagnosis of God's death, God's silence towards mankind, should therefore be understood as the loss of The Truth; a loss which hailed not nihilism, but the hopeful departure for new shores of a man bearing responsibility for himself.

Nietzsche's struggle against the obstinate history of truth was consistently continued by Foucault in his books.[1] Significantly, Foucault became well-known for a book which traced a part of this history of truth as the 'history of insanity in the age of reason'. Foucault, then, turned his attention to ostracized subjects and the various processes of exclusion, firstly for the simple reason of portraying the production of truth through a history or excavation of its 'trash'. 'The placement of true discourses (which, incidentally, change unceasingly) is one of the fundamental problems of the West. This history of "truth" – of the power inherent in those discourses accepted as true – remains entirely to be written' (DE 3/258). In this sense, Foucault wished to write the 'history of sexuality' not as 'a historical sociology of a ban' but as a 'political history of a production of truth' (DE 3/257) – something the

88

German title *Sexualität und Wahrheit* (sexuality and truth) rendered clearer.

Such a 'production history' of sexuality, extending back to Plato in its origins, acquires its political explosiveness from the fact that it describes truth in its emergence; thus what is acknowledged as normal is alienated through the revelation of its origins. In this way a genealogy of sexual morality joins in a game of truth which does not end with the 'truth' about the supposed truth. Foucault's concept of fiction should also be interpreted in this sense: The genealogies as 'anti-sciences' (DE 3/165) should not establish any new 'truths', but demonstrate ways towards the transformation of the earlier ones. Regardless of the various themes, Foucault remained true to this fundamental task which corresponded to Nietzsche's dictum of *Umwertung* (revaluation).

The work of the transformation, however, the revaluation, is itself already part of a valuation, or at least of an attempt to pursue science not simply as a 'discovery of truth' but as a 'surmounting of truth'. At precisely the point at which the scientist, in the interests of truth, withdraws to a neutral position, pretending that science can only be served thus, Foucault, by raising the problem of attitude, 'politicized' the intellectual's or the philosopher's role. This is nowhere so clearly seen as in his later work.[2] Inherent in the ethics of existence thematized in his last books is also the question of the intellectual's ethics; for thought itself, as the constant concern for the truth, is the condition for the modification and stylization of one's own life. For Foucault, there existed between the 'elaboration of the self by the self' and the ethics of the intellectual, an isomorphism upon which was based 'a studious transformation, a slow and arduous modification through a constant care of the truth' (DE 4/675). Here Foucault was also describing his own task as so-called intellectual; a task which was not reduced to the position of university type or academic, but which saw philosophy as an existential care of the truth rather than as a spiritual love of truth. 'The key to the personal poetic attitude of a philosopher is not to be sought in his ideas, as if it could be deduced from them, but rather in his philosophy-as-life, in his philosophical life, his ethos' (FR 374). For Foucault, philosophy as a lifestyle, as an expression of one's own biography,[3] was the precondition for the intellectual's task of making changes in the thought of others as well, and of providing, with his genealogical analyses, the know-how for such a transformation.

The philosopher should neither prescribe nor prophesy; he is much more a 'destroyer of evidences and universalities' (DE 3/268) than an adviser. His restless glance falls on the diagnosis of the present in order 'to shake up habitual ways of working and thinking, to dissipate conventional familiarities' (DE 4/676). Foucault saw it as philosophy's fundamental task 'never to consent to being altogether at ease with one's own evidences' (DE 3/787). The philosopher is an advocate of freedom in that he shows how, at a particular point in history, truths were *created*, which can be criticized and changed. 'It is one of my targets to show people that a lot of things that are a part of their landscape – that people think are universal – are the result of some very precise historical changes. All my analyses are against the idea of universal necessities in human existence. They show the arbitrariness of institutions and show which space of freedom we can still enjoy and how many changes can still be made' (TS 11). At the point where truth threatened to assume the form of a law and become regulation, Foucault began his critical questioning of the reasons. For him, the commitment of his philosophical life, his ethos, was an endless work of 'truth-telling', in order to oppose the conservative power which prescribed truth as creed and certainty.

THE PARRHESIASTIC SCENE

Nietzsche's *Redlichkeit* (honesty) and Kant's courage (*sapere aude*) can be comprehended as parts of an attitude which Foucault thematized in his final lectures on ancient technologies of the self as 'parrhesia' or 'truth-telling'. This parrhesiastic attitude was not only part of a widespread ancient way of life, but also reflected Foucault's own ethos as 'philosophy-as-life'. He who tells the truth is honest because he would not like to be false towards himself; he is courageous, because by telling the truth he exposes himself to a danger which under certain circumstances could put his own life on the line. In short, the parrhesiast is one who risks something by telling the truth.[4] For Foucault, however, the main stake in this parrhesiastic game of truth was not simply in the proclamation of the truth, but in the form of criticism practiced by the parrhesiast towards himself or his 'opponent'. A rule of the game here is that the truth-teller be in a subordinate position to his interlocutor; as, for example, a philosopher criticizing a tyrant, or a citizen criticizing the majority. Truth-telling only acquires its special form of criticism as a dare.

Since truth-telling is not reduced simply to pronouncement of the truth, but demands the art of criticism, parrhesia requires the speaker's knowledge of his own genealogy and status. 'More precisely, parrhesia is a verbal activity in which a speaker expresses his personal relationship to truth, and risks his life because he recognizes truth-telling as a duty to improve or help other people (as well as himself). In parrhesia, the speaker uses his freedom and chooses frankness instead of persuasion, truth instead of falsehood or silence, the risk of death instead of life and security, criticism instead of flattery, and moral duty instead of self-interest and moral apathy' (DT 8). For Foucault, the peculiarity of the ancient parrhesia lay in the fact that it occured outside any institutional framework, and did not therefore appear as a coded effect, but rendered possible a number of yet unknown effects. The singularity of the parrhesia consists in the truth, once it is released, opening up an uncertain risk for the speaker; in this sense Foucault also talked of an 'eruptive truth-telling'.[5]

For Foucault, the explosive nature of the parrhesiastic scene lay not simply in the voluntary game between a sovereign and the subject critical of his power, but primarily in the ethical and personal attitude of him who summons up the courage for truth and criticism. It is the subject's parrhesiastic alliance with himself which, for honesty's sake, summons the courage to pronounce the truth in spite of the possible consequences for life. In this way the parrhesiast, by virtue of his bravery and independently of his social status, shows the freedom of a vocal individual who is fully aware of his courage. Thus the ethics of parrhesia lays in its dangerous and free act.

The suggestion arises that Foucault implicitly associated the ancient practice of truth-telling with the modern critical attitude of the Enlightenment, and thus attempted to portray, beyond the epochal delimitations, an ethos which, as a problematization of one's own existence and as a 'philosophy-as-life', was present in each era to varying degrees. It is therefore not surprising that the verbal activity of parrhesia reflected the central definition of philosophy as art of life (*technē tou biou*), and became the focal point of Foucault's great theme of self-care (*epimeleia heautou*). For Foucault, truth-telling was a part of critical philosophical practice. In this sense, his books can be seen as 'parrhesiastic works', which attempted a critique of existing power relations and joined in the fashioning of the never-ending work of freedom. Foucault himself, who spoke as a 'philosopher' or an 'academic' at the Collège de France, brought 'into play a certain dramatic of the true discourse'[6] in that he did not simply carry the truth from the library to the lectern, but was himself the expression of his own ontology and his will to comprehend his present. The academic, intellectual experiment began with self-care and the philosophical task of bringing to light the genealogy, leading to the here and now, of one's own thought. Thus seen, the problematization of truth-telling is not to be separated from Foucault's effort to determine his own genealogy, his own status within modern philosophy.[7] Foucault clarified this parrhesiastic function of his philosophical work – his task as historian of thought was 'the analysis of the way an unproblematic field of experience, or a set of practices, which were accepted without question, which were familiar and "silent", out of discussion, becomes a problem, raises discussion and debate, incites new reactions, and induces a crisis in the previously silent behavior, habits, practices, and institutions. The history of thought, understood in this way, is the history of the way people begin to take care of something, of the way they become anxious about this or that – for example, about madness, about crime, about sex, about themselves, or about truth' (DT 47–8).[8]

SOCRATES' IRONY, DIOGENES' TRICKERY

In Foucault's view, Socrates and Diogenes embodied two forms of ancient truth-telling: the pedagogical strategy of a critical questioning and the provocative strategy of a critique of power. Both Greeks have in common that their critical attitude was the heart of an individual way of life and hence a philosophy as lifestyle in which Foucault's ethos can also be recognized. The irony of the one and the trickery of the other were living examples of a philosophical, ethically founded lifestyle; a lifestyle which questioned power in its different forms, constantly attempting, with the never-ending task of criticism, to modulate it and bring it back to its sensible limits. This critique of power and its potential abuse can only be undertaken, however, by someone who has first followed the Socratic imperative, taken care of himself and been concerned with his ontological harmony; in Foucault's words: 'ground yourself in freedom, through the mastery of yourself' (DE 4/729). In an ethics which problematizes the technologies of the self, Foucault saw at the same time the possibility, founded in freedom itself, of resistance to every form of one-sided power practice. In this sense, Socrates and Diogenes practised parrhesia, free and honest speaking.

Accounting for one's life is a lifelong process, not exhausted simply in the confession of personal cares and wishes, but which aims at the styling, the alteration of that life. This self-critical reflection of one's life should lead to 'whether you are able to show that there is a relation between the rational discourse, the *logos*, you are able to use, and the way that you live. Socrates is inquiring into the way that *logos* gives form to a person's style of life; for he is interested in discovering whether there is a harmonic relation between the two' (DT 61). The interrelation between a 'correct' use of one's own reason and the styling of one's own life had therefore a central place in the self-education demanded by Socrates. In this his philosophical concern was to achieve an agreement of words (*logoi*) and deeds (*erga*) and to avoid a discrepancy between what one says and what one does. Foucault also described this state as 'ontological harmony' (DT 63), in which an individual's reason (*logos*) and life (*bios*) harmonized, independent of his social or intellectual status. In this, Socrates' philosophy of life was in clear conflict with that of the sophists, who held fine discourses on subjects not directly connected to their own life. For Socrates, it was not truth itself as objectivized knowledge of no consequence to one's own life, which had priority, but rather it was the courageous life, the bios, which was 'the focus of Socratic parrhesia' (DT 64). Socrates' problem was the 'life truth' of an individual, 'how this relation to truth is ontologically and ethically manifest in his own life' (DT 65).

The Delphic oracle 'know thyself' was the call to strive for an ontological harmony between mind and life, soul and body. The first prerequisite for this task of self-knowledge was a critical attitude – Socrates' ironical and sceptical 'ignorance' – in order to resist both the sophists' flatteries and rhetorical arts of seduction, and one's own contradictions and self-deceptions.[9] 'Socrates' discourse requires that one overcome self-ignorance about one's own situation' (DT 66) by a critical questioning of the present truth. Serving maturity and life conduct, this care of one's own life and its fashioning was found in Socrates' pedagogical lessons. Socrates the parrhesiast also reflected the critical attitude of philosophy and hence Foucault's own ethos. His books should not be seen primarily as academic works, composed merely in the abstract service of science, but as parts of a life integrated in the games of truth. Bearing witness to this are, not least, Foucault's political deeds which complement his words.

An ethical attitude particularly represented in the figure of Diogenes was Cynicism; it gave greater emphasis to the relationship between philosophy and politics, called even more for parrhesiastic bravery and radicalized the Socratic parrhesia in its conception of the relationship between one's own life and the knowledge of truth.[10] Diogenes' provocative lifestyle was given expression above all through his 'permanent negative and critical attitude towards any kind of political institution, and towards any kind of nomos' (DT 67). He turned against collective habits, etiquette and institutional dependencies, pleading for self-sufficiency and independence. For that reason the Cynics' preaching seemed 'to have been directed against social institutions, the arbitrariness of rules, of law, and any sort of life-style that was dependent upon such institutions or laws' (DT 79). In contrast to Plato, the Cynics' fundamental relation to philosophy lay, however, not in a specific doctrine, but in the exemplary nature of their life. For Diogenes, the truth did not lie outside his life, but took form in the manner in which he led this life. In this respect Foucault saw the Cynics as being Greek through and through. For him, the fundamental characteristics of Cynic parrhesia were criticism, offence and participation in 'provocative dialogue' (DT 78). The Cynic was a truth which has become a living example, visible to the public and thus estranged from a 'specialist philosophy'. More important to the Cynics than a theoretical construct was to measure truth against one's very life, to make it the touchstone of the relationship of one's own truth. In the framework of ancient self-concern, however, this meant above all to be concerned with the nearest, everyday things, and through exercise (askēsis) to give one's life an individual style. In this manner the Cynic way of life was also a 'continuous exercise' (UP 73) in the constitution of oneself.

The main aspect differentiating Diogenes from Socrates was the circumstances of the dialogue: While the latter played the ignorant teacher, questioning the old truths, Diogenes was known as 'the dog'[11] whose main target was the pride of the sovereign, as is shown in Diogenes' famous conversations with Alexander.

Diogenes wished to injure, not to teach. Diogenes' parrhesia consisted above all in his tricky critique which limited the sovereign's power by shaming him with the reflection of his own immoderation. For Foucault, the parrhesiastic snub to the ruling power and its methods was the starting point for 'permanent and fundamental relationships' (DE 4/721) between philosophy and politics. Diogenes, by offering the picture of a modest and self-sufficient way of life and thus exposing the sovereign's hubristic style of leadership, entered a free provocative and courageous dialogue with power. In free conversation Diogenes craftily made Alexander explain himself and stood up to the sovereign with the example of his own life. In Diogenes' attack against Alexander's pride as ruler, Foucault's question as to how truth-telling confronts power is clearly expressed.

Foucault saw the critical tradition of occidental philosophy reaching back from Kant's question of Enlightenment to Socrates' critical discussions.[12] For precisely this reason he was interested in a 'genealogy of the critical attitude in Western philosophy' (DT 114). For Foucault, such a genealogy of morality extending back to antiquity was the attempt at a critique which asked why certain things were problematized at certain times. 'Why, for example, certain forms of behavior were characterized and classified as "madness" while other similar forms were completely neglected at a given historical moment; the same thing for crime and delinquency, the same question of problematization for sexuality' (DT 115). Foucault thus characterized his work since his early study *Madness and Civilization* as a genealogy of particular problems, as a 'problematization' (DT 114). In this it was not a question of some problem or other, but of a current problem which challenged the work of critical thought and the philosopher's truth-telling. Foucault expressly warned against believing, however, that in the case of such a problematization it was a question of an 'effect or consequence of a historical context or situation'. Instead it is 'an answer given by definite individuals' (DT 115) – a problematization based not in historical necessity, then, but in the practice of freedom. Foucault was alluding here to his own personal signature neither scientifically nor otherwise binding, which left each person free to share the results of his work and to open them for other critical approaches. In this sense, his project of problematization is itself only one possible answer, an 'invention', a product of thought which holds open the opportunity for its modification.

The genealogy of a problem is the comprehensible 'history of an answer – the original, specific, and singular answer of thought – to a certain situation' (DT 116). For Foucault, his critical philosophical task was provocatively, cynically and – in Nietzsche's sense – 'maliciously' to question, within the parrhesiastic scene of the present, the origin of a particular problem, in order to thus allow a political strategy of change. In this way, Socrates' irony, Diogenes' trickery, Nietzsche's honesty and Foucault's problematization are the personal signatures of a parrhesiastic tradition of Western thought concerned with the quintessential problem of philosophy: the games of truth.

7
Technologies of the Self

Foucault researched the portrayal of history which revealed the various ways that people in Western culture developed a knowledge of themselves. With the examples of medicine, psychiatry, punishment and other areas, he had tried to show that the institutions and so-called scientific discourses he examined are not something inevitable that must be accepted,[1] but can be analysed as 'very specific "truth games"' (TS 18); games which are based on concrete techniques, by which man strives to attain an understanding of himself. Here Foucault differentiated between four main types of technologies: '(1) technologies of production, which permit us to produce, transform, or manipulate things; (2) technologies of sign systems, which permit us to use signs, meanings, symbols, or signification; (3) technologies of power, which determine the conduct of individuals and submit them to certain ends or domination, an objectivizing of the subject; (4) technologies of the self, which permit individuals to effect by their own means or with the help of others a certain number of operations on their own bodies and souls, thoughts, conduct, and way of being, so as to transform themselves in order to attain a certain state of happiness, purity, wisdom, perfection, or immortality' (TS 18). In his late studies on a history of sexuality, beginning with the first volume *La Volonté de Savoir*, a book which was still concerned with the technologies of power, but which already cast doubt on power's one-sided, repressive ruling structure, Foucault had dealt with that fourth type of 'self-technologies'; those which are no longer connected to particular forms of knowledge or institutions, but which have validity *'in all societies*, whatever they are'.[2] Here the emphasis was no longer on technologies related to power and control, but on the technologies of the self as practices of freedom.

The critics' astonishment at Foucault's later change is unphilosophical,[3] because all his works are characterized by the continuity of an analysis of the games of truth, and thus revolve around a central problem of philosophical questioning: the problem of freedom. The fact that Foucault ultimately concerned himself with self-practices rather than with sexuality has already been addressed above. It is simply not sufficient to 'liberate sexuality', but to find out how freedom can be ethically problematized as a practice which comes from the individual himself; a practice which alone allows access to other forms of pleasure and relationships. The question then, concerns how freedom is *practised*, and not how one frees oneself. For freedom, as a given good, does not necessarily liberate one from a specific power relation (for example through divorce of a marriage humiliating for the woman). Freedom is not simply a right guaranteed by state or law (e.g. freedom of speech), but demands the ethical elaboration of technologies of mastery, which are based on the individual's relation to himself and others.[4] Foucault called this exercise of mastery connected to self-technologies 'governmentality' (DE 4/728), a term intended above all to prevent a conception of power and mastery which was limited to the master–slave antagonism. Instead Foucault saw 'governmentality' as characterizing an agonal relation, 'which is at the same time reciprocal incitation and struggle' (BSH 222), and hence is closer to the ancient idea of contest than the humanistic ideal of universal equality.

According to Foucault, freedom is 'the ontological condition of ethics', but 'ethics is the deliberate form assumed by freedom' (DE 4/712). Consequently, ethics is not simply a doctrine of moral desire and action, based on an abstract, as yet inanimate sense of freedom; rather, it begins with the individual's critical moral reflection on his life, in order to give him a certain conduct and attitude. Shaping one's own ethos and attitude, then, means elaborating a personal stylistics of existence which is visible in the way of life and mode of conduct. Ethics was not intended to be a general doctrine for everyone, but the form of reflection enabling each to lead his own individual life, producing a particular style and manner of being. Foucault was concerned neither with a uniforming rule, nor with finding a categoric imperative; rather, 'it is the unity of an attitude born of the individualization of moral action'[5] which represented for him the ethical challenge, a far cry from a theory of the subject. 'One's ethos was seen by his dress, by his bearing, by his gait, by the poise with which he reacts to events, etc.' (DE 4/714). Freedom assumes form in the manner in which a person is capable of giving his life a style, and how this style, this attitude becomes visible to others. Freedom is thus 'immediately problematized as ethos' (DE 4/714), and not as a humanistic ideal.

'Extensive work by the self on the self is required' for the individual's life 'to take shape in an ethos' (DE 4/714), that is, to become recognizable as a work of this individual, revealing his own unmistakeable style. It is not enough to get divorced, or to free oneself from anything; on the contrary, a care of the self is necessary to avoid the danger of foreign domination, and to be able to exercise freedom. In particular with the example of the ancient ethics of existence, Foucault attempted to show that self-relation and self-care have 'precedence ontologically' (DE 4/715), that participation in the city first required one to lead one's life in a reflective manner.[6] Both ethics and the practice of parrhesia described above, are only possible when the individual is in possession of his freedom. For this reason, the individual who is hindered in the mastery and conducting of himself has no ethics.[7] Ethics begins with a culture of the self as a cultivation of, and working on, the yet undefined material – springing from the innocence of becoming – of one's own life. Care of the self, then, is a lifelong endeavour to retain oneself, and to replace obedience and dependence with the courage for a self-responsible fashioning of one's freedom.

With his final studies on the technologies of the self, Foucault did not attempt to deny the problem of domination and potential abuse of power. Nevertheless he denied that the elaboration of individual ethics necessarily had to be linked to 'social or economic or political structures' (FR 350), or that one had to first 'free' oneself from these. On the contrary he saw, in self-care and the technologies of the self, the opportunity to undermine the omnipotence of large institutions through an individual who, unimpressed by them, is beginning to act on his own. Democratic institutions alone are no guarantee for freedom, but those people who act within them and are responsible for their functioning.[8] Here Foucault differentiated between two forms of power relations: (1) The rule and control mechanisms of the institutions creating a society's order; (2) the mastery relationship as self-reference in which a moderated use of power is problematized. With the ancient example of moderation, Foucault changed perspective and problematized, not the conception of one-sided, repressive power, but the relation of the individual concerned with his own intellectual and physical strengths. In the case of a critical self-care and an ontological knowledge of oneself, Foucault ruled out the danger of a hubristic use of power and exaggerated self-love, causing neglect of others.

For ethics as a practice of freedom meant the art of acting self-responsibly, and creating an ontological harmony through moderate dealings with one's own forces. The Delphic oracle 'know thyself' did not mean discovering the secret of oneself, but finding one's individual balance through knowledge of one's mental and physical limitations. Losing this exercise of moderation led to the tyrannical or slavish excess towards oneself and others; for the ancient understanding of sovereignty this meant the loss of one's freedom.

The fundamental aspect of self-constitution problematized by Foucault, and the possible technologies of the self which should constitute the sovereign subject, is askēsis, the work on oneself. The concept of askēsis assumes a key position in the understanding of a culture of the self: It differs not only in its ancient and Christian meaning, but also connects ethics with an aesthetics of existence. In a general, yet ancient, pagan sense, the term askēsis meant for Foucault a 'self-forming activity (*pratique de soi*)' (FR 355), understood as a work on oneself through which the individual bestows his life with a unique form and style. The technologies of the self were therefore essentially ascetic techniques which should enable one to be master of one's own behaviour. In this, ancient askēsis differed fundamentally from its Christian counterpart in the manner of self-relation: What was, for the Greeks, the elaboration and problematization of moderate ethics with respect to dietetics, economics and erotics, increasingly became, in Christianity, a morality of self-privation, and – with regards to sexuality – a hermeneutical work of self-deciphering. Opposed to an ancient ascetic elaboration of oneself as an ethics of existence was, in Christian asceticism, a cleansing hermeneutics of desire as attainment of 'spiritual salvation'. In Christianity, the ancient techniques of askēsis which were to be elaborated as a practice of freedom and free will and which problematized self-relation, underwent an encoding of conduct which became binding for all. The law's form ultimately dominated the ethical art of a voluntary self-forming activity.

Askēsis, familiar to us as a Christian defamation of the pleasures, had the affirmative meaning of a Socratic exercise. Obeying the Delphic oracle did not mean discovering one's pure, true self by condemning one's desires as sinful; it meant developing a sovereign, free individual through moderate dealings with ones pleasures. Socrates' much noted resistance of Alcibiades' seductive beauty does not demonstrate the baseness of pleasure, but the ancient ideal of self-mastery. For the correct reserve – that is, one corresponding to the principle of moderation – could only be achieved by a sovereign use of the pleasures;[9] thus, one avoided their excess which would be accompanied by the loss of control over oneself. The ancient definition of askēsis, which Foucault wished to reveal beyond Christian good and evil, meant an exercise and testing of oneself. In ancient morality mastering and leading oneself distinguished the free man, who was also worthy of leading others in the city.

Askēsis, according to this pagan understanding of sovereignty, is the work to be carried out on oneself. The ascetic attitude of Socrates was not the demand on Alcibiades to become chaste, but the pedagogical appeal to care for oneself. It is not sufficient to shine with the beauty of one's youth, but – according to the older and notoriously ugly Socrates – to become superior to one's pleasures and master of one's own life. Beauty is not reduced to Alcibiades' seductive appearance, but receives through Socrates' ascetic ethos a more comprehensive sense: only through a moderating conduct controlled by one's own reason can one succeed to the superior attitude as master of oneself, desirable also for others, and thus to an aesthetics of existence which does not place sole value on exterior beauty. This expresses the ancient will for form in contrast to the Christian search for meaning.

In Foucault's view, askēsis was far more than a mere technique of self-empowerment; it was an exercise in 'conditioning oneself', in the sense of altering and styling oneself, which lasted a whole lifetime. Foucault was not encouraging us to be self-satisfied, but to become a different person to the one we are. If pagan technologies as ascetic techniques appeared to him worth reproblematizing for the present, then it was with the aim of taking leave of a philosophy centred around the truth of the subject and replacing it with a virtual self capable of transformation. Instead of making a plea for a metaphysics of the merely hidden, and therefore discoverable 'true' self, and an identity-creating, norm-setting 'truth' of the subject, Foucault called for an art of living by way of transformation technique and for an inherently natural will for change. In his later work, detached from a Christian doctrine of salvation and a hermeneutical *Sinnstiftung* (creation of meaning), dethroning the dictate of both the *one* God, the *one* truth and their idols, Foucault announced the aesthetic impetus of his genealogical studies: man *is* not, he must *become*. This reveals what Desmond Bell referred to as Foucault's 'intellectual asceticism': His writings are the results of a philosophical exercise in thought, written with the intention of reopening the games of truth and decentralizing the supposed subject.[10]

'In the work of thinking on one's own history, philosophical askēsis should open the room of different thought. The *essay* is the living *body* of philosophy provided that the latter is askēsis, i.e. self-exercise in thought: Essay, that is the attempt at a modifying self-testing in the game of truth.'[11] Norbert Bolz specified Foucault's genealogical writings as ascetic essayism, thus emphasizing the aesthetic aspect over Bell's intellectual one. Foucault's essayistic writings – essayistic in the way they make an experiment of oneself – were the personal signature of a self-technology which invited other, not necessarily academic games of truth. Genealogy, by proving the contingency of the self precisely through its historical development, is enrolled in an aesthetic programme, a gay science. Foucault's genealogical work concluded by breaking the spell of the modern subject of desire, the 'sujet sexuel' and coincided with the – only seemingly – surprising attempt at a 'homosexual askēsis' (DE 4/165). Foucault saw the 'return' of the ancient constitution of the sovereign moral subject in self-relation, once pedagogically reflected in love of boys, in a social change which is still underestimated as the marginal theme of a 'social minority', and hence not viewed in its tendencial future-directed significance: the phenomenon of the gay ascetic, no longer identifiable as a *'sujet sexuel'*. For homosexual askēsis was, for Foucault, above all an affirmative, 'gay' self-exercise. In Nietzsche's words, the arcanum of the *Übermensch* (overman) in a culture of the self ran: 'Mich selber zu mir selber – zu verführen' ('Seducing myself – to myself') (3/360).

8

Aesthetics of Existence

Along with archaeology and genealogy, Foucault brought in the term 'problematization' in order to show his works as genealogies of particular problems. With regard to sexuality, this meant writing the genealogy of the hermeneutical subject of desire extending back to antiquity; that is, studying how sexuality could assume the form of the individual's particular truth about himself. However, as diagnostician of the present, Foucault was not interested solely in the constitutional conditions of the modern subject of desire, but also in the attempt at transgressing it. His late journey into antiquity originating in the contemporary problem posed by the interlinking of sexuality and truth was the attempt to create a new horizon of experience. For Foucault, writing the history of a problematization did not mean drafting a 'history of solutions' (FR 343), but rather, revealing the possibilities for its future transformation.

POLYMORPHOUS RELATIONSHIPS

In the first volume of *The History of Sexuality* Foucault expressed criticism of the so-called 'liberation movement' as a strategy for overcoming repression; thus he rejected Wilhelm Reich's concept[1] – functioning solely as the reverse side of sexualization – that the 'sexual revolution' promised liberation from puritanical repression. Nevertheless, Foucault did take note of a social phenomenon making itself apparent within the 'anti-repressive' mood at the end of the sixties, allowing him to problematize an ethics and aesthetics of existence right up to his death in 1984: the 'gay liberation movement'.[2] In the summer of 1969 a raid in the New York gay bar the 'Stonewall Inn' resulted in a militant clash between the police and homosexuals. From this time on a gay movement arose, gaining impetus mainly in North American and Western European cities, which demanded an end to social discrimination of homosexual men and women. The gay movement, however, did not function as

103

a rigid social institution, but was articulated rather as a new self-confidence among people for whose relationships no legitimate provision was made within the marriage- and family-based system of Western societies.

Since 1969, a gay 'subculture'[3] has been flourishing in the shadow of state institutions; a subculture whose lowest common denominator forms a monosexual, virile social structure, but which is beyond conventional sociological categories: from mechanic to manager, the so-called homosexual is a 'polymorphous pervert', precisely in the 'twisted' sense that he gives the lie to the psycho-analytical construct of human genital organization. In the 'subculture' and its 'sub-individuals' (DE 3/311), therefore, Foucault did not see the psychological characteristica and 'visible masks of the homosexual' (DE 4/165) supposed by a certain section of society, but the very variety and potential of a newly developing culture. This is no longer based on the legal-institutional and tradi-tional-ideological pillars of heterosexual marriage and family; it is founded instead on a voluntary ethics concerned first and foremost with the self, and leads not to legal alliances, but to a work on friendship.

Foucault was sceptical of the gay movement's political demands insofar as it often chanted the slogans of sexual liberation and thus confirmed the stereotype of the homosexual as a subject reduced to the different nature of his sexual desire. As long as the supporters of the gay movement remained 'all too caught up in the demand for the rights of their sexuality, in the dimension of sexology' (DE 3/321), it hindered the opportunity for new relationship forms which went beyond sex. For Foucault's problem was not the 'unleashing' of sexuality, but showing that homosexuality offers 'an historic opportunity to re-open affective and relational virtuali-ties, not so much through the intrinsic qualities of the homosexual, but due to the biases against the position he occupies; in a certain sense diagonal lines that he can trace in the social fabric permit him to make these virtualities visible' (DE 4/166).

With his last books Foucault was not so much intending a plea for homosexuality in the sense of favouring a certain sexual conduct, as attempting rather to highlight the 'diagonal' homosexual desire – non-integrable in the classic structures of marriage and family – as the starting point for a new 'relational culture'. In Foucault's opinion, the fact that homosexual ways of life are not institutionally fixed implied the need for their free ethical arrangement. In this respect and as demonstrated in *The History of Sexuality*, ancient Greek ethics was the attempt to pose anew the question of homosexuality for the present, thus delivering it of its character as pure 'liberation movement'; an attempt to find a 'principle on which' homosexuals and others could 'base the elaboration of a new ethics. They need an ethics, but they cannot find any other ethics than an ethics founded on so-called scientific knowledge of what the self is, what desire is, what the unconscious is, and so on' (FR 343). Precisely here lay an essential motive for Foucault's return to classical antiquity. The common ground between the pederastic model of the Greeks and modern homosexuality experienced primarily by adults, is that due to their institutional 'contrariness' both forms demand the willing, playful elaboration of relationships. In this the problem of homosexuality lies not in the peculiarity of a desire, but in the task of building diverse relationship structures, outside the 'extremely few, extremely simplified, and extremely poor' relationships of our 'legal, social, and institutional world', our 'institutions of lack' (DE 4/107).[4] Polymorphous, heterogeneous relationships were Foucault's affront on the monopoly of marriage and family.

By bringing forward the social restriction inherent in 'bio-politics' (HS 139), the problem of homosexuality demonstrates the possibilities both of breaking up the previous monopoly of the subject of desire and of beginning the invention of new forms of pleasure and communal life. Sexuality should no longer be a power which bestows truth and meaning, to be divided into 'normal' and 'perverse', but should be seen as a part of human conduct, as an expression of a physical and affective need. 'Sexuality is something that *we ourselves*[5] create – it is our own creation, and much more than the discovery of a secret side of our desire. (...) Sex is not a fatality; it's a possibility for creative life.'[6] By genealogically breaking the spell of 'sexuality', and attaining – from its hermeneutical, fatalistic depths – the free, still formless surface of a natural drive, Foucault pointed out the opportunity for a culture for which sex and the maintenance of the community was no longer legitimized by the monogamous, reproduction fixated 'elephant model' (DE 4/173), but in the voluntary, ethical foundation of friendship. Consequently, for Foucault, both the present-day problem and the historical opportunity of homosexuality did not consist in clinging to a deceptive 'liberation', but in working on the invention and fashioning of new forms of relationships. The focal point was not the idealistic community of the family, but friendship as a work of freedom.

On the one hand, Foucault spoke of homosexuality as an 'historical opportunity' (DE 4/166), on the other, warned against 'identifying with the masks of the homosexual' (DE 4/165). Above all, he rejected being taken for an advocate of a 'homosexual liberation movement', committing himself instead to looking beyond this 'liberation'. For Foucault, the historically developed differentiation between hetero- and homosexuality was not an acceptable necessity, but a reason for a fundamental questioning of the current pattern of desire. In order to give up the stereotype of the 'different' homosexual desire, and to avoid reducing it to a 'boring' (FR 340) sexual conduct, Foucault emphasized a terminological difference which clarified the divergence between mere sexual conduct and cultural achievement: 'We don't have to discover that we are homosexuals. (...) Rather, we have to create a gay life';[7] we have, he added significantly, to '*become*'. The rejection of the primarily 'scientifically' characterized term 'homosexual' in favour of an ethical use of the word 'gay'[8] is crucial to Foucault's observation that homosexuality – or more pertinently, 'gayness' – is an historical opportunity. He therefore saw the challenge of homosexuality in a gay lifestyle yet to be created rather than in the homosexual sex act itself. Hence, homosexuality is not an identity-forming profession of a particular type of desire, but something to be desired.

David M. Halperin took up this difference, criticizing the existing black-and-white terminology using a term which more strongly emphasized the process of creativity.[9] His use of the word 'queer', which can mean both 'gay' and 'strange, peculiar, odd', designates rather an 'eccentric positionality' than an attribute. Halperin defined this positionality as a non-conformity with that which is regarded as normal; a non-conformity not limited to homosexuals, but being 'in fact available to anyone who is or who feels marginalized because of her or his sexual practices'.[10] With this definition, Halperin is taking into particular account Foucault's lifelong attempt at rejecting the constricting mechanisms of identity formation ('I am homosexual.' 'You are criminal.' 'They are mad.') by explaining it genealogically, and replacing a domestically arranged certainty with the never-resting positionality of 'being different'.

Instead of 'discovering' the 'truth' about one's own 'sexuality', Foucault called for the invention of new forms of pleasure. Desirable was the 'desexualization of pleasure',[11] not the appropriation of a sexual identity, as has been shown by the hermeneutic problem of conferring identity and meaning which has become visible in the modern phenomenon of 'sexuality'. Foucault countered the discovery of 'sexual preferences' with imaginative, innovative practices with which physical pleasure par excellence – that is, without the stubborn fixation on its sexual origins – can be achieved: 'with very odd things, very strange parts of our bodies, in very unusual situations'.[12] The example of the sadomasochistic subculture (S/M) mentioned here by Foucault is *one* possibility of achieving a desexualization of pleasure through certain techniques. Such a 'gay culture will be not only a choice of homosexuals for homosexuals. It would create relations that are, at certain points, transferable to heterosexuals.'[13] S/M, from this perspective, is less a 'sexual practice' than the attempt to sensitize the body for new experiences in the use of pleasures. Furthermore the role-reversibility inherent in the sadomasochistic game is representative for Foucault's understanding of power *relations* as the 'intrinsic logic of a game of interactions, with its constantly changing margins of uncertainty' (CA 51). S/M is not a form of domination, but a game between free individuals, who, in the switch between subject and object risk the experiment of an uncertain, contingent 'limit-attitude' (FR 45).

Foucault also demanded this openness in the game for the social structures currently prevailing which still marginalize other forms of relationships and social life.[14] He pleaded for a new 'relational right',[15] which permitted all possible types of relationships, thus creating the precondition for a culture where 'other forms of pleasure, of relationships, coexistences, attachments, loves, intensities'[16] could be invented. In this way Foucault saw the 'problem of homosexuality' (DE 4/163), which once loomed on the horizon of the liberation movement, become a question of 'gay style':[17] With the creation of new relationship forms and lifestyles which differed from the institutionalized ones, gays brought to light the cultural virtualities and a different experience of culture.

Inherent in the 'gay lifestyle' which Foucault considered desirable is the ethical practice of that self-transformation, which finds expression, not in an ethical norm or an aesthetic ideal, but in the unique plastic of singular existence. However, Foucault was not looking for an identity-giving pattern for a 'ghettoized' gay community, nor imploring a 'return' to the circumstances of antiquity; he was trying to reformulate the problem of an 'homosexual askēsis' through the example of pagan ethics. For him there was 'one link between the ancient practices of self-mastery and contemporary homosexuality ... that both require an ethics or ascetics of the self tied to a particular, and particularly threatening, way of life'.[18] He was not interested in homosexuality as a special form of desire, nor was he searching for a subject buried in antiquity, which had only to be unearthed in order to be of use for contemporary ethics. Foucault saw Socrates' ascetic ideal as a central aspect of a homosexual way of life:

> Asceticism as the renunciation of pleasure has a bad reputation. But the askēsis is something else: it's the work that one performs on oneself in order to transform oneself or make the self appear that happily one never attains. Can that be our problem today? We've rid ourselves of asceticism. It's up to us to advance into a homosexual askēsis that would make us work on ourselves and invent, I do not say discover, a manner of being that is still improbable (DE 4/165).

Being gay, therefore, was not explicitly linked to a sexual way of life or identity; it was not the manner of identifying oneself as a 'homosexual' or 'heterosexual' object of desire. Rather, it was the tempering of a 'sexualized' life in favour of a culture of the self, in which the self is continually recreating itself, giving style to its character.

In Foucault's opinion, 'it is not necessary to be homosexual but it is necessary to be set on being gay. To be gay is to be in a state of becoming' (DE 4/295); he saw it as an art of transformation, of making a work of art of one's own life. If the ethics of a gay lifestyle is a way of permanently recreating new forms of subjectivity, and if the modelling of one's self into a living work of art is the starting point for a culture appearing in all its virtualities, then this 'body of development' (DE 2/140) also includes the flexibility and diversity of thought which emphasizes, not a static being, but the creative potential of becoming. The brilliancy of an aesthetics of existence replaces the desire to fog up life with meanings. Foucault, who had always refused to provide a programme or ready-made concept, intentionally left vague this transformation of the self, in which the illusion of an ideal self is destroyed. However little he spoke of a 'homosexual culture', which might lead to the assumption that it was already in existence, as little was the reanimation of a past ethics his concern. 'The programme must be empty' (DE 4/167).

ON FRIENDSHIP

Far more important for Foucault than the question of homosexual or pederastic preference was another trait in which the modern experience of homosexuality was linked to antiquity, and which provided an essential prerequisite for a culture of the self: 'mono-sexuality'. The concept of monosexuality illustrates that it is not sexual orientation which is decisive, but a social structure in which the sexes each have their own spheres and forms of living together. In his last two volumes of *The History of Sexuality*, Foucault described with particular clarity the extent to which antiquity was shaped by a monosexual society; a society which did not merely have the form of a 'patriarchal' power over women, but which was primarily determined by a virile ethics concerning the masculine community.[19] Foucault's view that the problem of homosexuality was decisively connected with the characteristics of a monosexual society is also shown in his observation 'that in America the society of homosexuals is a monosexual society' with 'a certain number of pleasures that are not of the sexual order' (DE 4/288–9). This 'number of pleasures' transcends the conventional clichés of a gay subculture as a mere satisfaction of sexual needs, concerning instead the organization of different cultural spheres which now trade under the label of 'monosexual': Sport, professional life, travel, gastronomy, advertising etc. In this 'relation of constant exchange' of American homosexuals, not characterized by tradi-tional family ties, Foucault saw a 'return of monosexuality'[20] (DE 4/289).

In an ethics and aesthetics of existence founded in a work on oneself, monosexuality is not necessarily another attribute of (homo)sexual relationships, but rather a question of friendship between two people of the same sex who, due to their voluntary, non-institutionalized bond, create new forms of togetherness which are to be made accessible in the practice of freedom. Here the art of friendship lies not in subjugation to a moral code or in the binding force of a contract, but in the open game between free indi-viduals, caring for themselves. It is not the sexual, economic appropriation of the other sex – which generally copies the one-sided principle of domination – but the voluntary arrangement of living together which preconditions the sovereignty and self-responsibility of both partners.

In Foucault's opinion, then, the problem of friendship should never be separated from an ethics of self-concern and the constitution to a moral subject of oneself. Thus a necessary precondition for conducting a friendship is that one first takes care of oneself and works at becoming one's own master. 'The care of the self is ethical in itself, but it implies complex relationships with others, to the extent that this ethos of freedom is also a way of caring for others' (DE 4/714). For becoming sovereign moral subject of oneself requires the experience and guidance of another, of an adviser, teacher or friend. Foucault also saw in this the significance of friendship with regards to his later expositions on the ancient practice of parrhesia: a friend tells us the truth about ourselves, through his criticism he protects us from overestimating ourselves; he creates distance and helps to give new order to our thoughts and deeds; he is a critical corrective for the daily work on oneself. In this way self-concern always goes hand in hand with care for others.

Friendship was not the place in which one subjected oneself to a particular 'relationship structure', but a point of exchange and common inventions. This problem of friendship which gained significance through Foucault's final studies on antiquity can be considered as indicating a possible continuation of his work: After a reconstruction of the historical origins of modern sexual ethics it appeared to Foucault increasingly important to reveal a culture of friendship based, not on love-thy-neighbour, but on an ethics of self-care. Foucault's succeeding works might well have pursued a genealogy of friendship as an understanding of its historical forms and conditions, illustrating once more his motive for a return to antiquity. Foucault supported his case with the hypothesis that, since the eighteenth century, a disappearance of monosexuality can be observed parallel to the development of political institutions, and that the affective, intensive and variable forms of monosexual friendship are being excluded by state institutions like military, administration or educational establishments due to 'reasons of state' – the allegedly superior interests of the community. At this historical interface Foucault saw the disappearance of friendship and the development of homosexuality into a social, political and medicinal problem as two phenomena of the same process. For the scandal of homosexuality is not its diversion from proper use of sexual conduct,[21] but the erection of intensive relationships, which disturb the order of bio-political reason and thus catch the state protected institutions in a contradiction.[22] (cf. DE 4/164). In contrast to legally fixed marriage concludable only between man and woman, monosexuality means being 'among men' or 'among women', living 'naked' and 'outside of institutional relations, family, profession and obligatory comradeship' (DE 4/164). In this sense Foucault saw the problem of homosexuality becoming more and more a problem of friendship.

In antiquity, friendship as the highest form of fellowship and as a social creation of a culture of the self, was based on the fundamental isomorphism between the Socratic imperative 'know thyself', and the agonal – and monosexual – relationship to the other. In this way the self-experience of the subject was reflected in the experience of the other, in a manner which observed the respective physical and affective state of the sexes. In Foucault's opinion the ancient experience of a monosexual friendship based on an ethics of existence conceived both by and for men, underwent a renaissance in the modern phenomenon of a gay way of life as a state of becoming, not limited to sexual practices. Aware of this modern problematic of gayness, friendship and monosexuality, Foucault traced back from the Christian-humanistic tradition to a pagan ethics of existence in self-relation and a sex specific isomorphism. An unstigmatized, unstereotyped experience of homosexuality should show how, even in antiquity, it was linked to the moral problem of the stylistics of an individual existence and was by no means a question of desire. Instead of responding to the modern problematic of a 'battle of the sexes' and its inability to abandon any differentiation between various forms of desire, Foucault exemplified through antiquity the richness of ethical questions which were not totalized in laws or institutions but which necessitated a work of freedom. Foucault's final work therefore, was not about a theory of the subject, but about the creation of new forms of subjectivity; he replaced normative ethics with a work of friendship to be fashioned in an open game.

The secondary literature on Foucault's later work virtually ignores the fact that his actual motive for a genealogy of the modern 'sexual morality' was the problematization of homosexuality as the basis for a comprehensive gay lifestyle;[23] that from this angle he brought to life the ancient attempt at an ethical and aesthetical way of life.[24] This topicality, clearly emphasized by Foucault himself through the example of a gay lifestyle, might also be the reason for the relative reticence within academic circles. Due to Foucault's notorious homosexuality and to later 'revelations' of other 'preferences', his final studies may have been seen as his own frivolous form of legacy – hence not to be taken seriously. This more especially, since Foucault died shortly after the publication of *The Use of Pleasure* and *The Care of the Self*. This academic shame, enveloping itself in the robes of science, is the expression of a common prejudice which fundamentally underestimates the explosive nature of Foucault's late work. For today, at the end of the twentieth century, and after two thousand years of Christian ethics, the problem of homosexuality can no longer be reduced to a bigoted tolerance towards him who feels differently, but should be considered as an aesthetic experiment. Here lies the challenge and the open horizon of a culture of the self which is being revealed in gay lifestyle – at the end of an era in which 'the idea of a morality as obedience to a code of rules is now disappearing, has already disappeared. To this absence of a morality, one responds, or must respond, with an investigation which is that of an aesthetics of existence' (DE 4/732).

9

I, Nietzsche

'I am simply a Nietzschean, and I try as far as possible, on a certain number of issues, to see with the help of Nietzsche's texts – but also with anti-Nietzschean theses (which are nevertheless Nietzschean!) – what can be done in this or that domain. I attempt nothing else, but that I try to do well' (DE 4/704). By thus acknowledging Nietzsche in an interview[1] only a few weeks before his death, Foucault expressed what had long been evident: His 'genealogy of problems, of problématiques' (FR 343) bore Nietzsche's signature. In a work comprehending such differing themes as madness and sexuality, continuity can therefore be discerned through the genealogical impetus originating in Nietzsche.

Foucault dated his 'fundamental Nietzscheanism' (DE 4/703) back to the year 1953. For him, reading Nietzsche was an escape from the unsatisfactory phenomenological theory of the subject and the start of a new relationship to philosophy as a critical attempt to write the history of thought and rationality. For Foucault, Nietzsche's 'witty, strange, and impudent texts' (DE 4/446), his coarse and unpolished 'mountain peasantness',[2] signified the possibility of another philosophical intensity lying beyond the bounds of old university tradition. Nietzsche's 'offhandedness' showed the way to recover from Hegelianism, and 'to exit from philosophy'.[3]

Instead of ignoring the traditional philosophical care of the truth, Foucault pursued its intensification: Not in the form of philosophical discourse and its problematization of the 'truth', but – in keeping with Nietzscheanism – in the role of the truth-teller, of the philosopher himself, diagnosing the present. Diagnosis by truth-telling does not mean uncovering The Truth but – in an anti-Platonic, anti-metaphysical, anti-Christian manner – to reveal its indetermination through the genealogical method. Genealogical diagnosis does not bring to light the essence of truth, but the contingency and innocence of becoming. For after God's death it is this innocence which must be rediscovered, and man who must be given back to himself. Hence genealogy is the method of the gay, atheistic anti-science, tracking down those overpowerful purpose- and sense-giving chimeras of previous science, thus breaking their metaphysical spell: the madness of reason, the vengeance of justice, the desire of sexuality. For Foucault, genealogy meant making God's death audible, so he can finally penetrate to 'the ears of men' (3/481).

NIETZSCHE'S PHYSIOSOPHY

In his most important essay on Nietzsche,[4] Foucault clearly devel- oped his mentor's genealogical viewpoint, separating it from a science of history which postulates progress and continuity in a place where breaches and discontinuities are apparent. By stirring up the 'sub-soil' of history, the genealogist deprives it of its 'ideal significations' and 'monotonous finality' (DE 2/136-37); he exposes historic truths as 'ancient proliferation of errors' (DE 2/139), which in their constancy became established as right. Rejecting an histor- ical meaning and the search for *Ursprung* (meaning here the fallacy of a fundamental 'initiality'), the genealogist, with no metahistori- cal zeal, researches in the shady area of *Herkunft* (descent, provenance), looks for 'subtle, singular, and subindividual marks' (DE 2/141) on the margins of crusades and revolutions. Genealogy as a diagnostic method is not seeking history's inherent soul, but studying its 'body of development' (DE 2/140). For this alone 'is the domain of the *Herkunft*. The body manifests the stigmata of past experience and also gives rise to desires, failings, and errors' (DE 2/142-3). For Foucault, the body was not a metaphor countering an evasive, metaphysical historiography, but a repeat of Nietzsche's physiological objections, which were not only directed at Wagner's 'sickening music' (6/419), an indigestible German cuisine (6/279–80), or Thuringia as one of the 'disastrous places' (6/283) of Nietzsche's physiology. Nietzsche's physiological glance ressembled far more that of a diagnosing doctor than the philosopher's viewpoint which omitted the facts of the body. In human moral judgements, Nietzsche saw above all 'a botched sign language', through which 'certain physiological facts try to inform the body' (10/284). Instead of a spiritual self-interpretation, he demanded from a future ethics the 'better ability to nourish oneself' and a smaller consumption – that is dietetic use – 'for one's own needs' (10/272). The body reveals the sign language of morality, which can essentially be read as 'a regulator in the conduct of the drives to one another' (9/348). The body also betrays who 'has overcome himself a few times a day, and who has always let himself go' (10/283). The 'great reason' (4/39): For Nietzsche, that meant listening to the nearest – 'the body, the nervous system, nutrition, digestion, and energies' (DE 2/149).

Nietzsche's diagnosis of present-day symptoms as 'aftereffects of some great dietary mistake' (3/485), and his demand from a future philosophy for the wisdom of the body as 'instinct for a personal diet', that is 'my own kind of health and weather, by the circuitous path of my head' (3/323), can only be irritating to those who seek comfort in the hermeneutical 'play of recognitions' (DE 2/147) and 'logical fictions' (5/18). Freeing himself from teleological principles, the seduction of words and their deceptiveness regarding the 'comprehensible nature' of being, Nietzsche questioned 'the moral effects of foods', asking for a 'philosophy of nutrition' (3/379). Nietzsche's future philosopher is he who is his own dietician, that is to say, the person who is his own doctor and pays heed to *his* health.

The 'body philosophizes' (10/226) was Nietzsche's unmetaphorical formula *against* 'the ignorance in physiologicis' (6/283) and *for* the future 'physiosoph' who places nutrition high on the list of priorities. For Nietzsche, an ethics of existence was inseparable from physiological circumspection which began not in devising a set of rules, but in a fundamental inquiry into correct nutrition – that is a nutrition appropriate for each individual. The 'ethical requirements must suit our body' (9/349), we must then, nourish ourselves so 'that we create ourselves in our own image' (10/470) – to name but a few of Nietzsche's insistent physiological demands. Nietzsche's attitude becomes most apparent at the point where he returns the crucified man, who believes himself possessed of an immortal soul, to the innocence of becoming beyond good and evil. Philosophy should no longer be a metaphysical dream of reason, an endowment of meaning which transcends the corporal; Nietzsche saw genealogy precisely as a physiological and historical inquiry into the laws and limitations, the origins of one's own bodily nature. The honesty of a gay science then, is found in its 'physical', and therefore irreligious, methods; methods which search not for the *sense*, the metaphysics of life, but for the *form*, the physique. Therefore, a future, 'truth-loving' philosophy should no longer -

metaphysically, idealistically – ask after 'the thing-in-itself', but examine 'to what extent truth can endure incorporation' – 'that is the question, that is the experiment' (3/471).

As a physiological interpretation of the 'weather signs of man' (10/433), and as a bridge to the overman, genealogy demands the body's rehabilitation from being the pawn of history, previously spurned by metaphysical intentions and purposes. Nietzsche's supposed 'nihilism' was aimed at one of the most constant axioms of philosophical history: at the identity of the subject, 'the subject-and-ego superstition' (5/11). For him, the body revealed 'a plurality with one sense' (4/39), which gives the lie to the unity of the ego. 'The body: ... place of the dissociation of the ego (attempting to adopt the chimera of a substantial unity)' (DE 2/143). While the ego mistakenly believes itself in possession of its sovereignty, the self triumphs as the body's great reason. Nietzsche's differentiation between 'ego' and 'self' highlights the rift between the philosophical pride of a 'subject' and the unrecognized wisdom of the body. The ego is 'the prompter of its concepts' (4/40), the belief in the 'thing-in-itself', it is responsible for the lifeless 'concept-mummies' (6/74) and 'concept-nets' (5/28) of philosophy which Nietzsche wished to silence before the honesty of the body convalescing from 'a metaphysician's ambition' (5/23). His recipe: create 'the meaning of the earth' (4/38) and banish the metaphysical shades through genealogy.

Nietzsche's genealogical experience was revealed precisely in that aspect with which he was later to be reproached. Implementing his own epistemological movement, his own genealogy, did not make him familiar with an authentic history identical to itself, but allowed him to appear amid the scenery of a 'theater without place' (DE 2/144), among the 'junk-sellers of vacant identities' (DE 2/153). Nietzsche's Western history is masquerade, travesty. From Jesus to Zarathustra, the fictitious Antichrist, it is peopled with figures displaying history's fundamental otherness and changeability. Donning oneself the masks of history, experiencing its idols and ideals through the study of genealogy, finally to become God oneself, 'because in fact I am every name in history'[5] – that is the ultimate dissolution of the subject, the unparalleled parody of world history. Nietzsche's century represented like none before the symptomatic freedom from commitment and the loss of an authenticity which until then had been guaranteed by God. This turned the nineteenth century into a farce – since then only 'God's buffoons' (5/157) are 'original' and as such Nietzsche remained his 'own sole contemporary', his 'own forerunner' (10/419, 555).

In his essay, Foucault revealed the motivation for Nietzsche's burlesque alienation of history: 'We may experiment with ourselves!' (3/294) This however, means nothing less than sacrificing philosophy's sacred cow, the epistemological subject, giving precedence to the 'movement of life' over the 'care of the truth' (DE 2/156) and thus introducing a colourful 'age of curiosity' (DE 4/108); an age which does not content itself with the truth, but which also has 'pleasure in the mask' (3/433). 'Get aboard the ships, you philosophers!' (3/530) was Nietzsche's call to embark on a gay science, quitting the mainland of the university. We have taken leave of dialectics, let us now invent style; the scholar has had his day, let us now start creating the overman! In 1879, with this pathos of the untimely, Nietzsche transformed from gloomy professor to gay scientist, from settled landlubber to nomadic seafarer, setting sail from Basel for yet unknown shores – travelling towards the free horizon on a perilous voyage to himself.

Nietzsche's 'physioaesthetic', anti-hermeneutical experiment has two sides which absolutely belong together: The aesthetic phenomenon justifying existence (1/17,47; 3/464), and the needful art of self-stylization (cf. 3/530). In these convictions, both owing to Greek antiquity, Foucault's Nietzscheanism is most audible and the aesthetic experiment inherent in genealogy most visible. God's death challenges the now self-responsible man to be serious about himself and reconquer his energies which had hitherto been channelled into a God. Here it should be remembered that God is only one of the names for Nietzsche's critique of Platonism, of the body-negating establishments of ideals. Nietzsche, the Antichrist *par excellence*, questioned belief in ego, meaning, purpose, logic, man, God, in short the entire Western order of things, erected since Plato. '*Nobody* is responsible for being there at all, … that he lives under these circumstances, these surroundings … That nobody is held responsible anymore, that the mode of being may not be traced back, … *that alone is the great liberation* – with this alone the innocence of becoming is restored … The concept of "God" was until now the greatest objection to existence … We deny God, we deny the responsibility in God: only *thereby* do we redeem the world.' (6/97) God's death – and the aphorism shows this quite clearly – signifies a shifting of weight from the hereafter of ideals and a human would-be reality to the here-and-now of life; from the salvation of the soul to 'the "salvation" of every single individual' (6/217). The great liberation following the twilight of the idols implies creating oneself from the contingency of one's existence. 'One thing is needful', Nietzsche constantly repeated to the deaf ears of his contemporaries: The new task after the death of God, to be achieved by 'long practice and daily work', is to '"give style" to one's character' (3/530).

Forever banished from God's garden of Eden, yet becoming aware of the 'gardens and plantations within us' (3/381), cultivating 'our temperament like a garden' (9/361), emulating those 'who are like a garden' (5/42): With this frequent use of the garden metaphor, Nietzsche tried to illustrate that one should care for oneself as for a garden, taming and styling the nature revealed within. For Nietzsche, working on and cultivating one's body and soul like the soil on which the seed should flourish, was a living image, not reducible to any theory, for the individual task of giving one's character a style. The person who oversees himself like a garden, planting one thing, removing another, watering and weeding, ultimately achieves that which, according to Nietzsche, is needful: self-contentment at the sight of 'stylized nature' (3/530). In this sense, Nietzsche saw the garden as an allegory for an aesthetics and ethics of existence; the art of gardening stood for the ability, with the aid of selected techniques, to bring the garden to bloom, to fashion a work from one's life. Nietzsche's lifelong plea also becomes clear here: in order to achieve a perspective free from the 'jaundiced eye of ressentiment'[6] (5/274), self-care is needed, in which one constitutes 'oneself as the worker on the beauty of one's own life' (DE 4/671). Nietzsche's 'needful thing', his task, was self-contentment through self-stylization, for 'the sight of ugliness makes one bad and gloomy' (3/530).

The garden is the body, the gardener a physiologist. Nietzsche never grew tired of repeatedly reciting this formula of his health and culture.[7] 'One must first persuade the *body*', not the mind or the soul. The 'right place is the body, the gesture, the diet, the physiology; the *rest* follows from that' (6/149). The 'rest' being the aesthetics of existence resulting from the care of the physique. 'Physiology of aesthetics' (5/356) means that the ideal of a beauty becoming visible in the individual has its basis in the physique, and not in an aestheticism. For this reason the rehabilitation of the body and of its own appropriate 'morality', promoting its health and form, was Nietzsche's main objection to Christianity. Instead of a

Christian asceticism, despising the body, Nietzsche wanted a return to ancient askēsis as a morality of moderation and daily exercise; an askēsis not hostile to the body, but which took its styling into consideration. Nietzsche's condition of culture was a 'naked-ancient' one rather than spiritualistic, and also bore in mind the 'lower requirements' (7/749) of the body.

FRIENDSHIP AND SELF-CARE

The fact that in Greek antiquity 'the men and youths were far superior in beauty to the women' (6/149) was fundamentally based in the care of the body's well-being, of one's own 'garden'.[8] For Nietzsche, virile ethics as seen in the example of antiquity was pivotal to an art of self-stylization directed at the body.[9] Although we may search in vain through Nietzsche's writings for the term 'monosexuality' employed by Foucault, nevertheless, Nietzsche left no doubt that the 'Greek culture of the classical era' was a 'masculine culture' (2/213), in which there was simply no place for the Christian model of the 'idealized sexual love' (3/295) still dominant today. 'The erotic relationship of the men with the youths was, to a degree we can no longer comprehend, the sole and necessary presupposition of all male education ... all the practical idealism of the Hellenic nature threw itself upon this relationship, and young people have probably never since been treated with so much attention and kindness or so completely with a view to enhancing their best qualities (virtus) as they were in the sixth and fifth centuries – in accordance, that is, with Hölderlin's fine maxim "for the mortal gives of his best when loving"' (2/213).[10]

The ancient philosophy was highly influenced by this living attempt of ethical arrangement of a beautiful, virile existence. Although Plato granted Greek culture the unsalutary dialectics owed to Socrates' plebian origins, thus paving the way for a Christian morality of the weak, Nietzsche reminded us of the wholly un-Christian, erotic origins of Platonic philosophy: The beautiful youths of Athens. 'Philosophy after the fashion of Plato might rather be defined as an erotic contest, as a further elaboration and internalization of the ancient agonistic gymnastics and of its *presuppositions* ...' (6/126). A presupposition for this, however, was not love of wisdom or the ideal of truth, but Plato's philosopher soul – transported into an 'erotic fever' by the beautiful youths of

Athens – which did not find peace 'until it lowered the seed of all exalted things into such beautiful soil' (6/126).[11] Behind philosophy as the love of wisdom was hidden in truth the love of beauty, behind the drive for knowledge – portrayed in Plato's *Symposium* 'as idealized aphrodisiac drive' – was shown the sensual enjoyment: 'always in pursuit of the beautiful!' (9/367) In this way, Nietzsche named unambiguously the agonal, predialectic impetus of Greek male-dominated society: that of boy eroticism subscribing to the image of the virile body, reflecting its needs. This eroticism expressed an ethical care, in which the 'man is seeking an idealized man' – not in the sense of being complemented by the other, but rather of 'perfecting their own best qualities' (2/272). Such an ethics necessarily excluded women; and friendship in which 'man stood beside man' (3/295) was the proper arena of the ancient ethos. The birth of philosophy in the garden of that virile pleasure to be moderated in favour of a stylistics of existence was the soil on which ancient culture stood.

Nietzsche had hoped to see his seed flourish in that same soil, and to meet his friend as the 'anticipation of the overman' (4/78). Here the overman is not to be imagined as any ideal type, but as the individual realization of a stylistics of existence. The overman is the manifestation of 'controlled multiplicity'[12] and stylized nature in the single individual, his 'best possible achievement' (*höchste Wohlgerathenheit*) (6/300). Friendship is the place where the aspiration to the overman takes shape in a 'fixing of oneself' (5/160) with one's best qualities. The motivation should be '*creating* something out of oneself that the other can behold with pleasure' – like a 'beautiful, restful, self-enclosed garden perhaps' (3/155), as Nietzsche added intimately. For the sake of one's own enjoyment and that of one's friend, one becomes the creator of oneself. 'You cannot groom yourself too beautifully for your friend: for you shall be to him an arrow and a longing for the overman' (4/72).[13] That was Nietzsche's 'law of the *double relation*',[14] his formula of ancient monosexual society, in which the man anticipated and reflected the completion of his own merits in those like him; friendship was the scene of virile self-knowledge, not only in an erotic sense, but also in a broader, namely physiological and aesthetic one. 'Let the future and the farthest be for you the cause of your today: in your friend you shall love the overman as your cause' (4/78). For Nietzsche remained alone, he never met *his* example of ancient friendship. Both Richard Wagner's case and that of other contemporaries could only convince Nietzsche that the 'time for me hasn't come yet: some are born posthumously' (6/298).

Nietzsche's will to become himself an overman, i.e. 'a well-turned-out person' (6/267), who, from the contingency of his life, creates a self-sufficing, self-affirming necessity, is visible throughout his *oeuvre*. Work on the overman was the effort to overcome modern man's weak personality. In order to prepare for the overman, Nietzsche as 'anti-teleologist' and 'labourer in physiology' (5/28) felt that his main task was to bring light to the continuing metaphysical realm of shadows after God's death and to prepare for the change in paradigms – the revaluation of previous values. From the authentic ego to the fictitious self, from man to overman, from Jesus to Zarathustra, from a metaphysics asserting 'aims' and 'purposes' to the 'inner cosmos' of a self-sufficing aesthetics of existence, from 'love thy neighbour' to 'know thyself', from marriage to friendship, from religion to life, from an 'objectivizing' science to a 'gay' self-knowledge, from a mind veiled in concepts to a 'cheerful digestion' (6/303), from 'theoretical evidence' to 'aesthetic pregnance',[15] in short: from sense to form. In this revaluation of modern values – which could be continued with further examples – it is not a question of simple negation merely aiming at the antithesis, but of the affirmative aesthetical project to convert the Christian promise of 'resurrection' into the Dionysian *amor fati* of recurrence.

Nietzsche opposed the promise of salvation in metaphysical, religious and more specifically also philosophical dogmas with 'the greatest weight' (3/570): The thought of eternal recurrence. Zarathustra's great question – 'Do you desire this once more and innumerable times more?' (3/570) – should become the greatest weight behind one's actions and replace the previous morality of aims and purposes; thus making man desire to become well disposed towards himself and life, in order 'to crave nothing more fervently than this ultimate eternal confirmation and seal' (3/570). This however means to justify and fashion one's life in such a way that it is at any time worthy of a repetition as an aesthetic phenomena, as a stylized nature; that one creates from the fluidity and plasticity of oneself a life which is memorable for others too, retaining its brilliance.

This was Nietzsche's greatest affirmation of existence, his greatest weight for all those acting self-responsibly and aware of the innocence of becoming – hence the way to the overman as a lawmaker and creator of himself. Thus seen, the overman was the greatest possible affirmation of oneself, the one who denied every-thing metaphysical in favour of this world and this, his life. That was Nietzsche's testimony to himself, *his* greatest weight. A person thus convinced about himself does not question philosophically in Plato's sense the true, the good, the beautiful, but asks physiologi-cally in Nietzsche's sense '*why* do you live here? ... What influence does this or that diet have on you?' (9/528) The main consideration of eternal recurrence, then, is not the attempt to replace the old creed with a new one, but an unconditional, affirmative *amor fati*, and the demand to fashion one's life as a work of art which makes one wish to experience it again and again. '*This life – your eternal life!*' (9/513) – that was what Nietzsche stressed most strongly, his ideal of 'recurrence' in precise opposition to 'resurrection'.

Twenty years before the publication of *The History of Sexuality* Foucault had already interpreted the modern cultural phenomenon of 'sexuality' in a Nietzschean way as a 'vicarious satisfaction' after God's death, and as the attempt to fill hermeneutically the 'ontolog-ical void' (DE 1/248) connected with this death. For this reason Foucault undertook the task of genealogically dethroning the idol 'sexuality' in order to attain an 'experience of the divine', (DE 1/239) an experience of the aphrodisiac pleasures, in which the 'sex-drive' is unmasked as 'prejudice' (9/207). Apart from its reproductive func-tion, which is the exception anyway and moreover should not be left to chance, the so-called sex-drive is without sense or purpose, hence by nature unfixed. Foucault proved once more that the modern commotion about sex is symptomatic of the inability to cope with God's murder, and 'that our path is circular and that, with each day, we are becoming more Greek' (DE 1/239; 11/679).

By intending, with his final studies on sexuality, a reproblema-tization of ancient morality, Foucault revealed the extent to which his thought followed Nietzsche's main physiological thread. Since Nietzsche, Foucault's work counts among the most logically consistent attempts to assist the preparatory work of ancient culture – so rudely interrupted by Christianity – to a late harvest after all, and to give Nietzsche's complaint a hearing.[16] In the higher, well-turned-out (over-)man, the aesthetics of existence prepared in antiquity should take shape and lead to a culture of the self, of friendship; a culture in which the innocent, undefined, unformed self elaborates a stylistics of existence from the theme of the body. For the belief in an authentic, 'actual' self was strictly rejected by Nietzsche, who demanded instead 'to *make ourselves*, to *fashion* a form from all elements' (9/361). It was in this sense Foucault interpreted Socrates' 'know thyself' as 'style thyself', thus making audible Nietzsche's dictum to give style to one's character. For Nietzsche, the task of self-fashioning had precedence even over knowledge, which he saw as, at most, a means to fulfil that task. In this way the overman represents Nietzsche's philosophy-as-life of taking the individual as an experiment. He is that model, that 'temptation' (5/59) to make of one's life a work of art. That was, for Nietzsche as for Foucault, the greatest challenge of a philosophy which did not provide a programme for everyone, but which called for a gay, cheerful, lively, colourful and varied work of self-stylization.

Conclusion

Foucault's later studies on an aesthetics and ethics of existence were the continuation of Nietzsche's genealogical project to prepare a revaluation of previous morality by analysing the degeneration – diagnosed as God's death – of that Christian order of values dating back to Plato's idealism. This revaluation was also an attempt to reconnect with ancient culture, to render its forgotten experiences visible for the present. In this Nietzsche saw the elaboration of a stylistics of existence as the crux of ancient moral reflection. Foucault's motive for recurring to antiquity is most clearly shown here. Nietzsche used the overman as a metaphor for the future creator of oneself, superior even to the Greeks, and, with an ethics of self-responsibility, attempted a care of the self. Foucault, on the other hand, put a name to the antichristian artist of life anticipated by Nietzsche: it is those who 'work on becoming homosexuals' (DE 4/163). Nietzsche's overman is 'gay' in the more original, not merely sexual sense of the word, and describes an aesthetics of existence: colourful, full of life, cheerful, bright. The message is addressed to those who take their ideal from themselves, ascribing a value to themselves on their own account (cf. 5/214); to those for whom the aesthetical and ethical arrangement of one's own life around the theme of the body is also the most important precondition for friendship. For Foucault, this ideal of a stylistics of existence was not manifested in those who lost themselves to the other, but in those who cared for themselves, worked on themselves. Foucault's target was the gay ascetic, the person for whom the desirableness of the other is inseparable from the pleasure in one's own 'garden'. Loving another in the same way that one would be the object of one's own enjoyment – due to the work on oneself – was not only the ancient formula of an ethical isomorphism characterizing monosexual society, but the highest form of a 'gay', cheerful affirmation; an affirmation which Foucault saw as becoming more and more apparent in the so-called 'gay culture' of the present day.

Foucault's recurrence to ancient experience in *The History of Sexuality*, though appearing at first glance to be his belated 'coming-out' and therefore an unserious – because unscientific – work, proves to be the consistent attempt to re-establish 'an order based on primeval times and which was prohibited by means of empty phrases':[1] an attempt to show that it is not the truth of an alleged sexuality which is relevant, but an ethics of friendship which begins with the individual's self-concern. For the 'primeval order' to which Foucault here refers means the right to be amongst men, and that in the most comprehensive, not merely sexual sense. From Christianity to the political institutions of the modern era, this right has been perverted by the monopoly of marriage and family, itself creating the problem of 'homosexuality', the 'homo-sexual' type. In this respect Foucault's experience of the ancient monosexual society consisted precisely in revealing the cultural virtualities of a 'gay' stylistics of existence no longer reducible to a sexual identity or to the poverty of societal institutions – thereby removing the stigma of anomaly from the modern problem of homosexuality.

In Foucault's view, the key factor of an ethics of existence in which the 'gay self' is characterized as something in a state of permanent becoming, that is, as something yet to be invented, was Nietzsche's 'one thing is needful' (3/530–1): a stylistics or an aesthetics of existence. This should hold itself aloof from any alleged purpose of the species 'man', and favour an ethics of the individual. Such an ethics required knowing one's own individual conditions of existence, 'nutrition, place, climate, recreation, the whole casuistry of selfishness' (6/295), in order to direct one's action from this standpoint, and to select the means for transformation, for fashioning oneself. In this apparently elitist ethics of the overman, in his 'gay' self-knowledge, Foucault saw the ethics of the gay ascetic, and at the same time his highest degree of maturity.[2]

Lastly it should be considered that Foucault's final books *The Use of Pleasure* and *The Care of the Self* are the visible results of such ethics, and fulfil – similarly to Nietzsche's *La Gaya Scienza* – an 'etho-poetic' function. They are his concrete autobiographical attempt to impart the never-completed reflection on the work of self-fashioning, both to himself and to those readers who, in keeping with Nietzsche's anti-hermeneutical interpretation, take their relationship with themselves as the starting point for a creative activity. In this sense, both Foucault's and Nietzsche's writings are similar to the literary genre of the essay, in which not science but self-knowledge is conveyed: The essay as assay and attempt, as 'an *askēsis*, an exercise of oneself in the activity of thought' (UP 9). Precisely due to this self-addressing, these books are not suitable for all eyes and ears – least of all perhaps for academic commentators.

Foucault once raised the point that 'perhaps we are too dedicated to commentary to understand what lives are' (DE 3/108).[3] To this, Walter Seitter made the following remark: 'Perhaps Foucault's scientific work is only worth so much, precisely as much as the suggestion – uttered outside academic circles – to say the word "life" with all the depth that modern age has burdened it with, in the plural form.'[4] It is here, in Nietzsche's perspective attitude, paying tribute not to theoretical evidence but to life, that Foucault's thought is most vulnerable, most open to attack by his critics. It should, therefore, be reiterated: Foucault's books are by no means to be interpreted as attempts at a continuing theorization; they are simply 'tool boxes' (DE 2/720), which should be used in a permanent work of improvisation and not in the development of scientific programmes. Thought is not formed in the ivory tower of academia but in the daily challenge which is life itself. As Nietzsche perceived it: 'Physiologically, not academically.'

A scientific thesis is a long way from being a universal truth. Defended by the game of truth from which it originates, it is lost with that game of truth yet to be invented. Every thesis, every theory remains the temporary approach of a thought enclosed and arranged within its own conceptuality. For this reason, a future philosophy should, in 'seeking out everything strange and questionable in existence' (6/258), show 'the extent to which things are immutable in character' in order to embark more decisively 'on *the improvement of that part* of the world *recognized as changeable*' (8/230). Instead of becoming entrenched and ending up as formulas of meaning, philosophy should take into account the heterogenity of the games of truth. The changeability expressed in the games of truth recalls the principle of becoming which is inherent in both life and body. For the precondition, the ethos for a philosophy manifested as gay science, is the variety and colourfulness of forms of existence which are revealed in each individual. Philosophy should therefore support the invention of new lifestyles, in which no limits are set to the imagination as long as its inventor's self-contentment and the cheerful expression of others is ensured.

Philosophy's challenge is to *create* new access to the games of truth. To this extent future philosophers should refrain from comforting themselves and others with the observation that that which 'is produced by scientific work should be important in the sense of "being worth knowing". And it is obvious that all of our problems lie here, for this presupposition cannot be proved by scientific means. It can only be interpreted with reference to its ultimate meaning, which one must accept or reject according to one's ultimate attitudes towards life.'⁵

Notes

INTRODUCTION

1. Michel Foucault: *L'Ordre du Discours*. Inaugural lecture at the Collège de France (2 December 1970). Paris, 1971, pp. 7–8.
2. *Le Monde* (6 April 1980), pp. I and XVII.
3. At this point we should draw particular attention to the subtitle of the French and German editions of *The History of Sexuality*, vol. 1: *La Volonté de Savoir* (the will to know), which is intentionally reminiscent of Nietzsche.

1   THE ART OF TEMPERANCE

1. For legal reasons the planned fourth volume of *The History of Sexuality* (*Les Aveux de la Chair*), dealing with the era of early Christianity, has not yet appeared in print. It is unclear whether it will ever be published.
2. 'One could say, of course, that psychoanalysis is a part of the tremendous growth and institutionalization of confessional procedures so characteristic of our civilization' (DE 3/235).
3. cf. Maria Daraki: 'Le Voyage en Grèce de Michel Foucault'. In: *Esprit*, April 1985, pp. 55–83. Renate Schlesier: 'Humaniora: Eine Kolumne'. In: *Merkur* 38 (1984), pp. 817–23.
4. cf. Foucault's remarks on this in DE 4/166, 289.
5. 'One must get rid of the subject itself, by ridding oneself of the constituting subject ...' (DE 3/147).
6. 'The ethical substance is like the material that's going to be worked over by ethics?' M.F.: 'Yes, that's it ... For the Greeks, the ethical substance was acts linked to pleasure and desire in their unity ... Sexuality is a third kind of ethical substance' (FR 353).
7. Max Weber: 'Science as a Vocation'. Trans. Michael John. In: Peter Lassman, Irving Velody (eds.): *Max Weber's 'Science as a Vocation'*. London, 1989, p. 30.
8. '... whereas I would like to use philosophy in a way that would permit the limiting of the domains of knowledge' (DE 4/707).
9. cf. DE 3/235.
10. Kenneth J. Dover: *Greek Homosexuality*. London, 1978. In his preface to the original Greek text of the *Symposium*, Dover clearly

emphasized that the 'Greeks did not consider homosexual relations incompatible with concurrent heterosexual relations or with marriage' (Plato: *Symposium*. Kenneth Dover (ed.). Cambridge, 1980. p. 3).

11. In a similar sense Foucault expressed himself with regards to his works: 'All my books ... are ... little tool boxes' (DE 2/720).

12. 'In the Californian cult of the self, one is supposed to discover one's true self, to separate it from that which might obscure or alienate it, to decipher its truth thanks to psychological or psychoanalytic science, which is supposed to be able to tell you what your true self is. Therefore, not only do I not identify this ancient culture of the self with what you might call the Californian cult of the self, I think they are diametrically opposed' (FR 362).

13. With this example we should compare an ethics of temperance with the present-day immoderation in the pursuit of sport activities: the cult of the body pursued in the widespread fitness studios pays homage to a muscular image of man which is in total opposition to an aesthetics of existence based on moderation. A comparable athletics, taken to extremes, can be seen in the 'Olympic idea' or rather, what is left of it. Immoderation does not only start with doping, which is merely the result of excessive demands on performance.

14. According to Nietzsche, for the Greeks love of boys had the function of limiting fertility, that is, it was a preventative against over-population and its negative side effects such as poverty and social unrest (cf. 9/514).

15. In order to clarify the difference between an agonistic ancient education – promoting at most city culture – and its state organized modern counterpart, Nietzsche should be cited once more: 'The preoccupation with the state should be diverted with an agonistic arousal – yes one should do gymnastics, write poetry – this has the additional success of making the citizens strong, beautiful and fine...young and old should stay together, not part, and retain the interest of the youths – otherwise the elders, separated from the boys, would have thrown their ambition onto the state, but with boys one could not talk of the state' (9/514–15).

2 A CULTURE OF THE SELF

1. For Nietzsche, Alexander not only embodied the decline of Greek culture, but was also the countertype of that self-care and need for self-enjoyment free of resentment which was so fundamental to this culture. In this he saw the essential reason for 'the necessity of counter-Alexanders who will retie the Gordian knot of Greek culture' (6/314).

2. Peter Lassman and Ronald Speirs (eds.): *Weber. Political Writings*. Cambridge, 1994, p. 316.

3 THE ROLE OF POWER

1. Hinrich Fink-Eitel: 'Zwischen Nietzsche und Heidegger: Michel Foucaults "Sexualität und Wahrheit" im Spiegel neuerer Sekundär-literatur'. In: *Philosophisches Jahrbuch* 97 (1990), p. 376 (my translation, H.N.).
2. cf. Foucault's 'definition' of power in 'Omnes et Singulatim: Towards a Criticism of Political Reason': 'Power is not a substance' (DE 4/160–1).
3. Here should be mentioned Gilles Deleuze's succinct definition, which corresponds to Foucault's: 'Power has no essence; it is simply operational. It is not an attribute but a relation: the power-relation is the set of possible relations between forces, which passes through the dominated forces no less than through the dominating, as both these forces constitute unique elements'. (Gilles Deleuze: *Foucault*. Trans. Seán Hand. London, 1988, p. 27.)
4. This raises the question as to whom or to what purpose the know-ledge of a theory of power should actually serve. Should it be an instrument of political power to prevent the hubris of power and its abuse, or should it be problematized on the level of self-techniques and as the will of the individual to give his life a beautiful form? In this case, however, it would no longer be a 'theory of power', but rather a practice of conducting one's life.
5. Fink-Eitel: 'Zwischen Nietzsche und Heidegger', p. 376.
6. Michel Foucault: *The Order of Things*. London, 1974, p. 387.
7. Later, in an interview in January 1984, Foucault commented that concepts like power are all 'ill-defined' and 'that one hardly knows what one is talking about'. He furthermore admitted that he too had probably not expressed himself very clearly on this subject, 'or used the right words' (DE 4/728).

4 THE PROJECT OF THE GENEALOGIES

1. Michel Foucault: *L'Ordre du Discours*. Inaugural lecture at the Collège de France (2 December 1970). Paris, 1971.
2. *Le Monde* (6 April 1980), pp. I and XVII.
3. 'Maurice Florence': Foucault, Michel 1926– In: Denis Huisman (ed.), *Dictionnaire des Philosophes*. Paris, 1984, pp. 942–4.
4. That part of the sentence in brackets comes from Foucault's assistant François Ewald.
5. cf. Renate Schlesier: 'Humaniora'. In: *Merkur* 38 (1984), p. 821 (my translation, H.N.). Foucault vehemently rejected this accusation of nostalgia: '... one should totally and absolutely suspect anything that claims to be a return ... there is in fact no such thing as a return' (FR 250).
6. Paul Veyne: *Comment on écrit l'histoire suivi de Foucault révolutionne l'histoire*. Paris, 1979, p. 231.

7.   ibid., p. 204: 'He is the first completely positivist historian.'
8.   Gilles Deleuze: *Foucault*. Trans. Seán Hand. London, 1988, p. 1.
9.   Desmond Bell: 'Michel Foucault. A Philosopher for all Seasons?' In: Desmond Bell (ed.): *History of European Ideas* 14 (3). Special Issue, Foucault. May, 1992, p. 336.
10.   Clare O'Farrell: *Foucault: Historian or Philosopher?* Basingstoke, London, 1989, p. 39.
11.   Foucault himself raises this question, posing it through a fictitious adversary in *L'Archéologie du Savoir* (1969): 'In any case, you have promised to tell us what these discourses are that you have been pursuing ... history or philosophy?' (AK 205).
12.   Clare O'Farrell: *Foucault*, p. 130.
13.   Gary Gutting also expressly drew attention to the fact that Foucault's primary goal was to understand the present, not the past. Only by bridging the gap to the present do his historical studies reveal their effects and become the political instrument of a transformative work which transcends mere knowledge about the past. cf. Gutting: 'Michel Foucault: A User's Manual'. In: Gutting (ed.): *The Cambridge Companion to Foucault*. Cambridge 1994, p. 10.
14.   cf. Dreyfus' and Rabinow's succinct definition in BSH 106.
15.   James W. Bernauer and Michael Mahon: 'The Ethics of Michel Foucault'. In: *The Cambridge Companion to Foucault*, p. 148.
16.   The extent to which Foucault's work should be seen as a 'Nietzschean project of genealogies' (DE 4/704) will be dealt with in a later chapter concerning the affinities of these two philosophers.
17.   Paul Rabinow: 'Modern and Counter-modern: Ethos and Epoch in Heidegger and Foucault'. In: *The Cambridge Companion to Foucault*, p. 203.
18.   This explanation refers to the subject but not to the social context which will be more closely defined in the final chapters of this study.
19.   Michel Foucault: 'About the Beginning of the Hermeneutics of the Self: Two Lectures at Dartmouth'. In: *Political Theory* 21 (2). (May 1993), p. 202.
20.   Desmond Bell interpreted the criticism of Foucault's books prior to his studies on an 'aesthetics of existence' as a 'relativising and nihilistic impact of his genealogy'. (Desmond Bell: *Michel Foucault: A Philosopher for all Seasons? History of European Ideas* 14 (3). Special Issue, Foucault. Oxford, 1992, p. 343). Nietzsche had already been accused of this attitude of the eternal sceptic, because he neither could nor wanted to fulfil the expectations from philosophy to announce universal truths: For this was in contradiction to Zarathustra's doctrine of becoming master of oneself.
21.   The less appropriate English translation of the book's title, *Madness and Civilization*, indicates an exclusively socio-critical context, whereas the original French title already announces the genealogical-philosophical direction of Foucault's studies.
22.   The subtitle of *Madness and Civilization – A History of Insanity in the Age of Reason* – highlights the central philosophical problem of Foucault's genealogies of the mad, criminal or perverse subject: It is

the question about reason concerning the historically formed rules of the games of truth, its process of exclusion and acceptance from which the ruling knowledge is constituted.

23. 'What struck Foucault was the manner in which the act of confining human beings was taken as something perfectly natural, as a procedure whose legitimacy was self-evident' (Karlis Racevskis: 'Michel Foucault, Rameau's Nephew, and the Question of Identity'. In: D. Rasmussen (ed.), *The Final Foucault*. Chestnut Hill, 1989, p. 139.

24. Michel Foucault: *Discipline and Punish. The Birth of the Prison*. Trans. Alan Sheridan. New York, 1977, p. 30.

25. A more exact investigation, not possible here, would have to attempt to show in what way Foucault's genealogy of the hermeneutical subject of desire was also a criticism of psychoanalysis. In this respect genealogy is the opponent of hermeneutics.

26. 'I reject a certain a priori theory of the subject ...' (DE 4/718).

27. Foucault: 'About the Beginning of the Hermeneutics of the Self', p. 202.

28. Bell: *Michel Foucault*, p. 343.

29. At the conclusion of this work, however, an 'answer' will be given with respect to a social phenomenon which Foucault viewed not as a promise, but as a challenge.

30. Bob Gallagher and Alexander Wilson: 'Sex, Power and the Politics of Identity. Interview with Michel Foucault'. In: *The Advocate*. Los Angeles, 1984, p. 27.

5 MODERNITY AS AN ATTITUDE

1. This chapter is principally based on the following texts of Foucault: (1) *'What is Enlightenment?'* In: Paul Rabinow: *The Foucault Reader*. New York, 1984, pp. 32–50; (2) 'Qu'est-ce que la critique? [Critique et Aufklärung]' In: *Bulletin de la Société française de philosophie* 84 (2) (April–June), pp. 35–63.

2. 'What does one call postmodernity? I am not in the know' (DE 4/446).

3. cf. also CA 47, in which Foucault considers the question of Enlightenment as being applicable 'to any moment in history', a question of the 'relations of power, of truth and of the subject'.

4. cf. David R. Shumway: 'Michel Foucault'. In: David O'Connell (ed.): *Twayne's World Authors Series. French Literature*. Boston, 1989, p. 156.

5. This statement referred to the Greeks, but can certainly be seen as one of those aspects of ancient morality which Foucault believed could be reactivated.

6. Pierre Hadot's 'fear' that Foucault's prospect was a new form or version of dandyism for the end of this century expresses an academic surprise and reserve towards the theme of a 'culture of the self' which is often met with. A new form of dandyism is less to be

'feared', however, than the fact that there is a fundamental conflict in continuing academic discussion about Foucault's final studies and their particularly apparent attempt to tear philosophy – as a life practice and stylistics of existence – away from its institutional establishment. This, however, can scarcely be solved in the form of an academic dispute. No contribution to the secondary literature will be able to fix Foucault's aesthetics of existence in an 'academic' manner; nor can this particular work fulfil such a claim. Aesthetics of existence is, by definition, not visible in books, but in life itself. (cf. Pierre Hadot: Refléxions sur la Notion de 'Culture de Soi'. In: *Michel Foucault, Philosophe*. Paris, 1989, p. 267.)

7. cf. Habermas, who wrote of the 'played through melody of a confessing irrationalism'. (Jürgen Habermas: 'Genealogische Geschichtsschreibung: Über einige Aporien im machttheoretischen Denken Foucaults'. In: *Merkur* 38 (1984), p. 747; my translation, H.N.)
8. Michel Foucault: Interview with Stephen Riggins. In: *Ethos* 1 (2), Autumn 1983, p. 8.
9. Jürgen Habermas: *Theorie des kommunikativen Handelns*. Frankfurt/ Main 1981.
10. In *The Birth of Tragedy* Nietzsche had named the tragic position precisely distinguishing man from animals – on the one hand making him painfully aware of death, on the other indicating his chance for freedom and the uniqueness of an aesthetical self-determination.

6   THE CARE OF THE TRUTH

1. It is precisely Foucault's attitude towards the Western dictate of truth that was criticized by Habermas as 'irrational'. At this point, however, the academic discussion ends and the scientifically irreducible question of the attitude towards life begins. Put bluntly: one is either Nietzschean or Hegelian.
2. One explanation for Foucault's concern for his own ethos – which can only be mentioned as speculation here, but is nevertheless probable – could be the awareness of his approaching death during the writing of the succeeding volumes of *The History of Sexuality*. Using himself as an example he demonstrated the importance of self-concern and thus identified himself with a tradition of thought which aimed at style/ethos instead of truth/knowledge.
3. 'Each of my works is a part of my own biography. For one or another reason I had the occasion to feel and live those things' (TS 11). cf. Nietzsche's remarks that ultimately everyone creates 'his own biography' (2/323), records his own 'mémoires' (5/19).
4. The following quotations of Foucault on the problem of parrhesia mainly derive from the text *Discourse and Truth. The Problematization of Parrhesia* (DT).
5. *Das Wahrsprechen des Anderen: Zwei Vorlesungen von 1983/84.* Ulrike

Reuter, et al. (eds.). Trans. Ulrike Reuter, Lothar Wolfstetter. Frankfurt am Main 1988, p. 33.

6. ibid., p. 39.

7. Here it should be remembered that for Foucault 'modern philosophy' was not simply a certain level of recognition of philosophy as a science, but the attempt to create a personal attitude, a lifestyle.

8. This list precisely corresponds to the chronology of those themes problematized by Foucault.

9. The attitude embodied in the sophists was not an exclusively ancient phenomenon; it can also be transposed as the attitude of the modern academic, whose 'ontological disharmony' becomes recognizable in the discrepancy between his own ethos and theoretical work. Nietzsche's critique of the scholar was also aimed in this direction.

10. In an interview he gave me in April 1996 in Paris, Daniel Defert, Foucault's life companion, underlined the fact that there is a strong affinity between Foucault's ethos and the Cynic attitude. The manner in which Diogenes made from his life, on the one hand a long-term exercise (askēsis), and on the other a scandal against the spirit of 'conservative values', is much closer to Foucault's philosophy than Socrates with his exaggerated concern for the truth. For this reason, Defert was disappointed in Didier Eribon's biography, which reduced Foucault's life to a 'harmless academic career'; he was also annoyed at James Miller's biography and its ridiculous idea of a sado-masochist with a death-wish.

11. Cynical is derived from the Greek *kynikós* and means, roughly, 'dog-like'.

12. Foucault doubtless had this affinity between the problem of Enlightenment and Socratic parrhesia in mind, as is shown in an interview of May 1978 (cf. CA 58).

7 TECHNOLOGIES OF THE SELF

1. 'There is *always* a possibility, in a given game of truth, to *discover* something else and to more or less *change* such and such a rule and *sometimes even the totality of the game of truth*' (DE 4/725–6) (my italics, H.N.). The possibility of the complete revaluation of the game of truth can also be applied to the culture of the self problematized by Foucault, and thus the dissolution of a Christian hermeneutics of the self manifest in the psychoanalytical game.

2. Michel Foucault: 'About the Beginning of the Hermeneutics of the Self: Two Lectures at Dartmouth'. In: Political Theory 21 (2). (May 1993), p. 203 (my italics, H.N.).

3. Instead of seeing a contradiction between the earlier and later works, Norbert Bolz held Foucault's various studies as 'questions of growing genealogical intensity' (Norbert Bolz: *Stop Making Sense*. Würzburg, 1989, p. 110; this and the following quotations from Bolz's book are my translation, H.N.). This intensity is not a forward-

moving process in the evolution of a theory-structure, but rather a genealogical 'going back' in order to analyse one's own thought and being in the contemporary games of truth.

4. For a woman breaking free from her husband's power abuse and her economic dependence on him, divorce represents only the beginning of a freedom which still has to be fought for, and which ideally has her own sovereignty as its goal. The price of freedom is a lifelong work to be undertaken on oneself.

5. Bolz: *Stop Making Sense*, p. 111.

6. This reveals the difference between pastoral power and what Nietzsche termed the 'slave morality' of Christianity's 'love-thy-neighbour' on the one hand, and on the other the ancient ethos which ignored slave status and saw 'the ethical principle of its permanence' (DE 4/715) in self-care. Power is first and foremost problematized in self-relation, not in opposition to the other.

7. The accusation crops up again and again, that Foucault was pursuing a socio-Darwinian even fascistic sounding glorification of the strong, sovereign individual, which blots out the reality of the weak and those in need of protection. The ontologically more relevant self-relation however, consisted precisely in an opposing principle: To find out one's own limits and tasks, in order to be worthy and capable of the responsibility towards others, including those dependent on help. Throughout his life, Foucault was concerned with the ethico-philosophical problem of responsibility – towards oneself, the other, the truth, power – not smug vanities. Why else the efforts at a genealogy of what we are today?

8. The culture of the self could also be contrasted with the term 'nation of culture': Of the latter there is no sign, in view of the dominance and reducing of democratic legitimization to economic questions. Since the end of the Second World War the anachronism of national thought has become increasingly evident; the politics of modern states echoes the economic fluctuation, and is consequently ethically soulless. Foucault's reproblematization of an ancient self-culture shows that it is not the concept of nation that should be redefined, but the perception of culture as an ethics based primarily in the reflection of personal lifestyle.

9. The plural reminds us that it is not solely a question of 'sexual' pleasure but also of eating and drinking, that is, a question of nutrition and diet. Foucault had pointed out that early Christianity too was far less concerned with sex – 'the problem was food, food, food' (FR 340). Through this basic example it becomes clear that 'ascetic' means a correct, temperate use of the pleasures, and not absolutely no use at all.

10. Desmond Bell: *Michel Foucault: A Philosopher for all Seasons? History of European Ideas* 14 (3). Special Issue, Foucault. Oxford, 1992, p. 340.

11. Bolz: *Stop Making Sense*, p. 115.

8 AESTHETICS OF EXISTENCE

1. 'I feel that the scheme of Reich should be abandoned completely' (DE 3/397).
2. The term 'gay liberation movement' used here signifies mainly the political battle against sexual discrimination and is not the expression of a *Weltanschauung*. The gay movement was never a fixed institution with which homosexuals might identify in a similar way as with a political party. On the contrary, it reflects the variety of lifestyles whose smallest common denominator is pleasure – in the wi(l)dest sense – in one's own sex. The spirit of a unified movement conjured up even by the 'gay movers' themselves is an ideological fuss and contrary to Foucault's demand that the programme had to be empty (cf. DE 4/167). 'Movement' here, then, means that something is in a state of becoming and forbids the conception of a unification which confers identity. This is also demonstrated by the yearly processions of gays and lesbians organized in numerous cities throughout the world, which have rather an aesthetical-carnivalesque character than a vulgar-political one. The colourful processions convey a way of life, not a political conviction.
3. The lesbian counterpart of this subculture should by no means be excluded. It should be considered however, that the ethical problem of self-stylization is based on a physiological order, and not a scientific principle or a theory of the 'subject', and hence cannot be considered independently of one's own sex. Foucault himself did not withdraw to a theoretical gender-neutral position, convinced that there is an isomorphism between the elaboration of an aesthetics and ethics of existence and the sex of an individual. The consequence of this is the problematization of a virile ethos (appearing, especially to women, one-sided and misogynous). In this sense, this work is also limited to the problem of male self-relation, reminding readers of Foucault's reference to Lillian Faderman's book *Surpassing the Love of Men* (cf. DE 4/166, 289 and Michel Foucault: 'Sex, Power and the Politics of Identity'. In: *The Advocate*, Los Angeles, 1984, p. 29).
4. Michel Foucault: 'The Social Triumph of the Sexual Will'. In: *Christopher Street* 4 (1982), p. 38.
5. My italics, H.N.
6. Foucault: 'Sex, Power and the Politics of Identity', p. 27.
7. Ibid., p. 27.
8. The original meaning of 'gay' is affirmative: cheerful, joyful, colourful, full of life. The attribute 'gay' therefore conveys strongly the conception of a feeling for life, an attitude towards life. It can be similarly seen in colour symbolism: Pink became a symbolic colour of the gay movement, because it was a reminder of the homosexual concentration camp victims of the Third Reich, who were stigmatized with the 'pink triangle'. The rainbow flag, on the other hand, with its colour spectrum, counts as one of the affirmative symbols and reflects the sense of the word gay – colourful.

9.   David M. Halperin: *Saint Foucault*. New York, 1995.
10. Ibid., p. 62.
11. Foucault: 'Sex, Power and the Politics of Identity', p. 27.
12. Ibid., pp. 27-28. Together with Foucault's own comments regarding S/M experiments, Hervé Guibert's novel in particular (*A l'ami qui ne m'a pas sauvé la vie*, Paris, 1990) saw to it that Foucault was discredited as a 'sexual desperado' (*Der Spiegel* 14, 1993, p. 226). Further impetus was given to this form of critique by the biography *The Passion of Michel Foucault* (London, 1993). The author, James Miller – as father of three sons, raised above all suspicion and belonging to those people who get 'squeamish over having a tooth filled' (ibid., p. 377) – attempted with hermeneutical passion to construct a connection between Foucault's ethos, his S/M practices and a conscious dicing with an AIDS-related death (cf. also Halperin's strong reply, in *Saint Foucault*, to Miller's frail conjectures, pp. 126–85).
13. Foucault: 'The Social Triumph of the Sexual Will', p. 39.
14. Foucault named, as the most important obstacle to a 'rich, relational' world also including gay and lesbian lifestyles, the fact that dealing with and 'administering' it would be very complicated (cf., 'The Social Triumph of the Sexual Will', p. 38). This argument agrees with his observations on late antiquity, where the so-called 'elephant model' soon dominated 'because it was connected to a social transformation which included the disintegration of the city-states, the development of imperial bureaucracy and the increasing influence of the provincial middle-class' (DE 4/173). It might be investigated, through the examples of the non-recognition of homosexual relationships or the prejudice against illegitimate children, how much the inflexibility of state administrative structures and their control functions are still ideologically based on the 'elephant model'; a model which, above all in the course of a 2,000 year predominance of Christian ethics, has led to a cultural reality which still serves conservatism as a justification for the status quo. The disappearance of national identity and an increasingly urban culture could be indications for a possible reversal of this development.
15. Foucault: 'The Social Triumph of the Sexual Will', p. 38.
16. Sylvère Lotringer (ed.): *Foucault Live (Interviews, 1966–84)*. Trans. John Johnston. New York, 1989, p. 144.
17. *Politics, Philosophy, Culture: Interviews and other Writings of Michel Foucault. 1977–84*. Lawrence D. Kritzman (ed.). New York, London 1988, p. 292.
18. Arnold I. Davidson: 'Ethics as Ascetics: Foucault, the History of Ethics, and Ancient Thought'. In: Gary Gutting (ed.): *The Cambridge Companion to Foucault*. Cambridge, 1994, p. 126.
19. At this point Foucault took into consideration that there would also have been close monosexual relationships between women (cf. DE 4/288). There were hardly any testimonies at all to these relationships, let alone from the women themselves. Instead, therefore, of concluding Foucault's attitude to be misogynous, 'feminist' critics would do well not to persist in justifying themselves through the

negativity of male dominance, but rather to care for themselves in an affirmative manner.

20. It is remarkable how the gay lifestyle, catching the institutions in a contradiction (cf. DE 4/164), produces a 'reversal' of previous valencies: Running through all nations – i.e. supranationally, it makes a 'travesty' of national values, that is, those values going back to Christian pastoral authority. Today, for example, there are the 'gay games' as a counterpart of the 'Olympic Games'; the legal recognition of gay/lesbian partnerships will also only be a question of time, that is, a consequence of this continuing transformation. The gay-lesbian 'doublings', from now on characterized by monosexuality, seem to run parallel to the loss of previous national identification and to be characteristic of all societies: Not only institutions, but also nations are 'caught in contradiction'. From this it becomes clear what makes being gay desirable for one and threatening for another. For a continuing 'gay revaluation' of the predominating morality leads sooner or later to the confirmation of Foucault's observation of American conditions: namely to a monosexual society.

21. Here it should be remembered which two 'purposes' – in opposition to ideological-modern 'bio-politics' (HS 139) and reasons of state – Nietzsche attached to love of boys in antiquity: prevention of over-population and diverting the mature men from the state (9/514–15). With regard to the first purpose, one should bear in mind that the Greek's pagan morality is more than 2,000 years distant, and draws attention to the unstoppable growth of present-day humanity, in which the 'barren homosexual' is still felt to be a provocation. Nevertheless, when homosexual couples wish to address themselves to the supposed social responsibility of 'reproduction', the ruling morality, legitimized as state authority, refuses them the right to adoption, instead supporting arbitrarily the procreation of anybody; in other words the so-called heterosexual majority, in whom the often ill-considered desire for offspring may be criticized. These considerations could be continued into the dispute over abortion, in which the present moral ambiguity becomes visible. Whilst for the Greeks a 'removal of the fruits of an unfortunate coitus' (9/476) seemed unproblematic, today's abortion debate cannot be conducted without 'Christian-humanist' indignation. Revealed in the themes of abortion, adoption or homosexuality – in short that which was criticized by Foucault as 'bio-politics' – is the interrelation of a continuing Christian morality with modern reasons of state. In this respect Foucault's works can be seen as an attack on the 'herd morality' already repeatedly denounced by Nietzsche and as a plea for '*many* free individuals' (9/476) – thus turning the 'problem of homosexuality' into a gay, polymorphous stylistics of existence.

22. This 'gay reversal' of existing social structures led Norbert Bolz to interpret Foucault's final studies as the invocation of the 'dandy of revolt' (Norbert Bolz, *Stop Making Sense*. Würzburg, 1989, p. 114), thus emphasizing the political volatility of gay lifestyle instead of the triviality of the sexual act. In a seminar at Berlin's Free University

(Summer 1988) Bolz reiterated Foucault's observation on the return of monosexuality and a cultural 'revaluation' connected with it: Nietzsche's 'impending return of the Greek spirit' (6/314) can be seen in the urban sign of a gay self-fashioning.

23. A typical example of this ignorance – often characteristic of academia's self-image – is the work of Wilhelm Schmid, whose index does not even list the heading 'homosexuality'. (Wilhelm Schmid: *Auf der Suche nach einer neuen Lebenskunst*. Frankfurt/Main, 1991) In the 400-page book, Foucault's motive is touched on, at best. Norbert Bolz, on the other hand, in an essay of only six pages, published two years earlier, clearly recognized Foucault's motivation for a return to antiquity ('Ästhetisierung der Existenz'; In: *Stop Making Sense*, pp. 110–15).

24. Norbert Bolz even spoke of Foucault's 'Wiederholung antiker Existenzästhetik auf der Spitze der Postmoderne' ('repetition of ancient aesthetics of existence at the height of postmodernity'; ibid., p. 110).

9 I, NIETZSCHE

1. This interview was conducted by Gilles Barbedette and André Scala on 29 May 1984, four weeks prior to Foucault's death. ('Le Retour de la Morale'. In: *Les Nouvelles littéraires*, Paris, 1984, pp. 36–41, also DE 4/696–707).

2. *Foucault Live (Interviews, 1966-84)*: Sylvère Lotringer (ed.). Trans. John Johnston. New York, 1989, p. 153.

3. Ibid., p. 153.

4. Michel Foucault: 'Nietzsche, la Généalogie, l'Histoire'. In: *Hommage à Jean Hyppolite*. Paris, 1971, pp. 145–72; also DE 2/136–56).

5. Nietzsche wrote this sentence on 5 January 1889 in his final letter to Jakob Burckhardt. There has been much speculation on Nietzsche's 'madness'. The 'truth' about Nietzsche's final breakdown is far more than the mere result of his 'parody' of history in which he finally even became God. The shattering incident in Turin, Italy which preceded Nietzsche's mental derangement can also be seen in another light – it was the compassionate gesture of a desperately lonely man, seeking comfort by hugging an old nag.

6. Nietzsche used the French word in the sense of a 'suffering from embitterment', as a 'feeling of bitter resentment', thus criticizing a Christian 'herd morality' of the weak, hostile to life and body.

7. One century of secondary literature has succeeded in transforming Nietzsche's body into spirit. Even Alexander Nehamas' outstanding study is toned down by the fact that its title – *Nietzsche: Life as Literature* (Cambridge/Mass., 1985) – suggests Nietzsche's stylistics of existence should be primarily considered as a literary self-fashioning, thus allowing the physiologist to vanish behind a mere literary figure. For Nietzsche, however, philosophy was first and foremost a

self-forming activity, the way to *his* personal diet. Only thus, as a 'Verzeichnung' (listing) of his way of life, as an individual 'note-book', does writing acquire its mnemotechnical significance for oneself and other readers. Foucault forcefully described this difference with the ancient example of *hypomnemata* (cf. FR 363–7). Nietzsche's books are – as is clearly expressed in *Ecce homo* ('And so I tell my life to myself', (6/263)) – the *listing* of the way one searches for one's individual pattern, creates one's individual lifestyle, simultaneously serving as a helpful example for those – not everybody – 'who are looking for their patterns' (9/206). Nehamas' characterization 'Life as Literature' would be an appropriate title for a study on Jean-Paul Sartre – but not on Nietzsche.

8. Here those accusations – not to be silenced by a footnote – of 'fascistic glorification of the body' and 'contempt for the physically fragile' – might make themselves heard. The body, stylized by daily work, should primarily serve, not the display of power and contempt for the weak, but joy in oneself, giving delight to the senses of others. Styling oneself as one's own object of joy and pleasure was the aesthetic, not fascistic telos of ancient-virile askēsis. (Cf. David M. Halperin's understanding differentiation in *Saint Foucault*, pp. 115–18.)

9. A visit to any museum with a collection from antiquity impresses on the mind the extent of the Greek 'passion for naked *male* beauty' (3/152).

10. There are few places in Nietzsche's work which so clearly defend ancient erotics against the modern 'chatter about the Greeks' (3/152). In the meantime, the question as to whether ancient relations will return in the form of a monosexual society, but without that antinomy of the boy which was so problematic for the Greeks, must remain unanswered. The weather-signs of the present revealed by Foucault seem to anticipate this, but the resulting weather is still a long way off. Perhaps future generations will look back with laughing amazement at today's problematic of a 'coming out'.

11. Regardless of the different interpretations of Plato's attitude to love of boys, one should keep in mind that 'there can be little doubt that homosexual response was the most powerful emotional experience known to most of the people for whom he [Plato] was writing'. (Kenneth J. Dover (ed.): Plato's *Symposium*. Cambridge, 1980. p. 5).

12. Nehamas, *Nietzsche*, p. 7.

13. Here one should recall Socrates' famous introductory words to the *Symposium*: 'I'm going to the house of a good-looking man; I had to look my best' (Plato: *Symposium*. Trans. Alexander Nehamas and Paul Woodruff. Indianapolis, 1989, p. 3). Plato's *Symposium* shows very nicely the ancient problematic between friendship and a stylistics of existence, and is far from deciphering Eros' 'secret of desire', as many other interpretations imply.

14. 'The style should be appropriate to you regarding one particular person to whom you wish to express yourself' (letter from Nietzsche to Lou von Salomé, Tautenburg 8/24 August 1882).

15.   Norbert Bolz, *Stop Making Sense*, Würzburg, 1989, p. 130.
16.   'The whole labor of the ancient world *in vain*: I have no word to express my feelings about such an enormity' (6/247).

CONCLUSION

1.   Michel Foucault: 'Wächter über die Nacht der Menschen'. In: Hans Ludwig Spegg (ed.): *Unterwegs mit Rolf Italiaander. Begegnungen, Betrachtungen, Bibliographie.* Hamburg, 1963, p. 48 (also DE 1/231).
2.   On the question as to his plans for the future, Foucault sincerely and unpolemically replied to his amazed, incredulous critics, that he would now take care of himself (cf. FR 342). At this point one could voice the suspicion that Foucault's greatest adversaries, perhaps, are those who are not capable of caring for themselves; that is, those by whom Foucault's (and Nietzsche's) self-care are most misunderstood.
3.   *Le Nouvel Observateur* 629, 1976, p. 83.
4.   Walter Seitter: 'Ein Denken im Forschen. Zum Unternehmen einer Analytik bei Michel Foucault'. In: *Der große Durchblick: Unternehmensanalysen.* Berlin, 1983, p. 93 (my translation, H.N.).
5.   Max Weber: 'Science as a Vocation'. Trans. Michael John. In: Peter Lassman and Irving Velody (eds.): *Max Weber's 'Science as a Vocation'.* London, 1989, p. 18.

Bibliography

Foucault's books have given rise to a secondary literature which in all probability has still not reached its full extent. Michael Clark's bibliography, published one year before Foucault's death, already listed 729 titles. If we were to compile an updated bibliography, including everything that has been written about Foucault since then, Clark's list would be lengthened considerably.

The most important archive of works by and about Foucault is the 'Centre Michel Foucault', currently situated in the Bibliothèque du Saulchoir (43 bis rue de la Glacière, 75013 Paris). Here can also be found many of the recorded lectures given by Foucault at the Collège de France or at Berkeley. The quality of the tapes unfortunately is poor, due to frequent playing.

In view of the numerous publications concerning Michel Foucault's *oeuvre* and the continual appearance of new publications on the international book market, the following bibliography can only be a selection. Like the many-faceted work of Foucault himself, the amount of secondary literature is evidence to the fact that there will never be a unified and final history of his thought – nor is this to be desired. Today, writing about Foucault should mean accepting, beyond all boundaries of academic convention, Foucault's challenge for a 'transformation of the frames of thought' (DE 4/110); learning to grasp truth not as a certainty but as a process of becoming. Thus every book which follows Foucault's various tracks in one or another direction is a single, temporary attempt at a restless and nomadic thought process – one which, arguably, can be traced back to Nietzsche.

A) WORKS BY MICHEL FOUCAULT

About the Beginning of the Hermeneutics of the Self. Two Lectures at Dartmouth (transcribed by Mark Blasius and Thomas Keenan). In: *Political Theory*. 21 (2) (May 1993), pp. 202–27.

An Interview: Sex, Power and the Politics of Identity. Interview by
Bob Gallagher and Alexander Wilson. In: *The Advocate*. Los
Angeles, 1984, pp. 26–30, p. 58.

Andere Räume. In: *Aisthesis. Wahrnehmung heute oder Perspektiven
einer anderen Ästhetik.* Trans. Walter Seitter. Leipzig 1992, p. 34–46.

Das Wahrsprechen des Anderen: Zwei Vorlesungen von 1983/84. Ulrike
Reuter, et al. (eds.). Trans. Ulrike Reuter, Lothar Wolfstetter.
Frankfurt am Main, 1988.

Discipline and Punish. Trans. A. M. Sheridan Smith. London, 1977.

Discourse and Truth: The Problematization of Parrhesia. Transcript of
six lectures in English. Joseph Pearson (ed.). Evanston, 1985.

Dits et Écrits. 1954–1988 (Bibliothèque des Sciences humaines). 4
volumes. Édition établie sous la direction de Daniel Defert et
François Ewald avec la collaboration de Jacques Lagrange. Paris,
1994.

Foucault Live (Interviews, 1966–84): Sylvère Lotringer (ed.). Trans.
John Johnston. New York, 1989.

Foucault, Passe-Frontières de la Philosophie (an interview by Roger
Pol-Droit, 20. 6. 1975). In: *Le Monde.* 6 Sept. 1986, p. 12.

Freiheit und Selbstsorge. Interview 1984 und Vorlesung 1982. Helmut
Becker, et al. (eds.). Trans. Helmut Becker, Lothar Wolfstetter.
Frankfurt am Main, 1985.

Histoire de la Sexualité, I: La Volonté de Savoir. Paris, 1976.

Histoire de la Sexualité, II: L'Usage des Plaisirs. Paris, 1984.

Histoire de la Sexualité, III: Le Souci de Soi. Paris, 1984.

La Gouvernementalité. In: *Magazine littéraire* 269 (1989), pp. 97–103.

Le Retour de la Morale. Interview by Gilles Barbedette and André
Scala. In: *Les Nouvelles littéraires.* Paris, 1984, pp. 36–41.

L'Ordre du Discours. Leçon inaugurale au Collège de France (2 Dec.
1970). Paris, 1971.

Mental Illness and Psychology. Trans. Alan Sheridan. New York, 1976.

Michel Foucault on Attica. Interview with John K. Simon (April
1972). In: *Telos* 19 (Spring 1974), pp. 154–60.

Nietzsche, Freud, Marx. In: Gayle L. Ormiston, Alan D. Schrift
(eds.): *Transforming the Hermeneutic Context: From Nietzsche to
Nancy.* New York, 1994, pp. 59–67.

Omnes et Singulatim: Vers une critique de la raison politique. In: *Le
Débat* 41 (Paris, 1986), pp. 5–35.

Photogenic Painting. In: *Critical Texts: A Review of Theory and
Criticism* 6 (3). Trans. Pierre A. Walker. New York, 1989, pp. 1–12.

Politics, Philosophy, Culture: Interviews and other Writings of Michel

Foucault, 1977–1984. Lawrence D. Kritzman (ed.). New York, London, 1988.

Politics and Ethics: An Interview. In: Paul Rabinow (ed.). *The Foucault Reader*. New York, 1984, pp. 373–80.

Polemics, Politics, and Problemizations: An Interview with Michel Foucault. In: Paul Rabinow (ed.): *The Foucault Reader*. New York, 1984, pp. 381–90.

Qu'est-ce que la Critique? [Critique et Aufklärung] (lecture and conversation, 27 May 1978.) *Bulletin de la Société française de philosophie* 84 (2) (April–June 1990), pp. 35–63.

Qu'est-ce que les Lumières? In: *Magazine littéraire* 309 (1993), pp. 61–74.

Structuralism and Post-Structuralism: An Interview with Michel Foucault by Gerard Raulet. Trans. Jeremy Harding. In: *Telos* 55 (Spring 1983), pp. 195–211.

Technologies of the Self. In: *Technologies of the Self: A Seminar with Michel Foucault*. Luther H. Martin, Huck Gutman, Patrick H. Hutton (eds.). Amherst, Mass., 1988, pp. 16–49.

The Archaeology of Knowledge. Trans. A. M. Sheridan. London, 1972.

The Birth of the Clinic: An Archaeology of Medical Perception. Trans. A. M. Sheridan. London, 1973.

The History of Sexuality: An Introduction. Trans. Robert Hurley. Harmondsworth, 1978.

The History of Sexuality: The Use of Pleasure. Trans. Robert Hurley. London, 1992.

The History of Sexuality: The Care of the Self. Trans. Robert Hurley. London, 1990.

The Order of Things: An Archaeology of the Human Sciences. London, 1974.

The Political Technologies of Individuals. In: *Technologies of the Self: A Seminar with Michel Foucault*. Luther H. Martin, Huck Gutman, Patrick H. Hutton (eds.). Amherst, Mass., 1988, pp. 145–62.

The Social Triumph of the Sexual Will: A Conversation with Michel Foucault. Trans. Brendan Lemon. In: *Christopher Street* 4 (New York, 1982), pp. 36–43.

Truth, Power, Self: An Interview with Michel Foucault (25 Oct. 1982). In: *Technologies of the Self*, as above, pp. 9–15.

Wächter über die Nacht der Menschen. In: Hans Ludwig Spegg (ed.): *Unterwegs mit Rolf Italiaander. Begegnungen, Betrachtungen, Bibliographie*. Hamburg, 1963, pp. 46–9.

Madness and Civilization. A History of Insanity in the Age of Reason. Trans. Richard Howard. London, 1967.

Was ist Aufklärung? Was ist Revolution? In: *die tageszeitung.* Berlin, 2 July 1984.

B) WORKS ABOUT MICHEL FOUCAULT

Améry, Jean: Wider den Strukturalismus. Das Beispiel des Michel Foucault. In: *Merkur* 27 (1973), pp. 468–82.

Arac, Jonathan (ed.): *After Foucault. Humanistic Knowledge, Postmodern Challenges.* New Brunswick, London, 1988.

Auzias, Jean-Marie: *Michel Foucault. Qui suis-je?* Lyon, 1986.

Bahr, Ehrhard (ed.): *Was ist Aufklärung? Thesen und Definitionen.* Stuttgart, 1981.

Barker, Philip: *Michel Foucault. Subversions of the Subject.* New York, 1993.

Baudrillard, Jean: *Oublier Foucault.* Paris, 1977.

Becker, Helmut: *Die Logik der Strategie: Eine Diskursanalyse der politischen Philosophie Michel Foucaults.* Frankfurt am Main, 1981.

Bell, Desmond (ed.): Preface/ Michel Foucault: A Philosopher for all Seasons? In: *History of European Ideas* 14 (3). Special Issue, Foucault. Oxford, 1992, pp. 329–46.

Bell, Vikki: *Interrogating Incest: Feminism, Foucault and the Law.* London, 1993.

Bernauer, James W.: *Michel Foucault's Force of Flight: Toward an Ethics for Thought.* New Jersey, London, 1990.

Bevis, Phil; Cohen, Michèle; Kendall, Gavin: Archaeologizing Genealogy. Michel Foucault and the Economy of Austerity. In: *Economy and Society* 18 (1989), pp. 323–45.

Blanchot, Maurice: Michel Foucault as I Imagine Him. In: *Foucault. Blanchot.* New York, 1987, pp. 61–109.

Bolz, Norbert: *Stop Making Sense!* Würzburg, 1989.

Boswell, John: *Christianity, Social Tolerance and Homosexuality: Gay People in Western Europe from the Beginning of the Christian Era to the Fourteenth Century.* Chicago, 1980.

Bouchard, Donald F. (ed.): Michel Foucault. *Language, Counter-Memory, Practice: Selected Essays and Interviews.* Trans. Donald Bouchard and Sherry Simon. Ithaca NY, 1977.

Bourdieu, Pierre: Le Plaisir de Savoir. In: *Le Monde,* 27 June 1984.

146 *Bibliography*

Boyne, Roy: *Foucault and Derrida: The Other Side of Reason.* London, 1990.

Brede, Rüdiger: Aussage und Discours: Untersuchungen zur Discours-Theorie bei Michel Foucault. In: *Europäische Hochschulschriften, Philosophie,* vol. 173. Frankfurt am Main, 1985.

Burchell, Graham, et al. (eds.): *The Foucault Effect: Studies in Governmentality (with two lectures by and an interview with Michel Foucault).* London, 1991.

Carroll, David: *Paraesthetics: Foucault, Lyotard, Derrida.* New York, London 1987.

Caruso, Paolo: *Conversazione con Lévi-Strauss, Foucault, Lacan.* Milano, 1969.

Clark, Michael: *An Annotated Bibliography: Tool Kit for a New Age.* New York, London, 1983.

Cook, Deborah: *The Subject finds a Voice. Foucault's Turn toward Subjectivity.* New York, 1992.

Cooper, Barry: *Michel Foucault. An Introduction to the Study of his Thought.* New York, 1981.

Cousins, Mark and Hussain, Athar: *Michel Foucault.* London, 1984.

Dane, Gesa, et al. (eds.): *Anschlüsse. Versuche nach Michel Foucault.* Tübingen, 1985.

Daraki, Maria: Le Voyage en Grèce de Michel Foucault. In: *Esprit,* April 1985, pp. 55–83.

Dauk, Elke: *Denken als Ethos und Methode: Foucault lesen.* Berlin, 1989.

——: Stille Post: Zum Königsweg der Foucaultrezeption. In: *Lendemains* 54 (1989), pp. 103–9.

Davidson, Arnold I.: Ethics as Ascetics: Foucault, the History of Ethics, and Ancient Thought. In: *The Cambridge Companion to Foucault.* Cambridge, 1994, pp. 115–40.

Dean, Mitchell: *Critical and Effective Histories: Foucault's Methods and Historical Sociology.* London, 1994.

Deleuze, Gilles: Désir et Plaisir. *Magazine littéraire* 325 (October 1994), pp. 59–65.

——: *Foucault.* Trans. Seán Hand. London, 1988.

Dews, Peter: Foucault and the French Tradition of Historical Epistemology. In: *History of European Ideas* 14 (3). Special Issue, Foucault. May 1992, pp. 347–63.

Diamond, Irene (ed.): *Feminism and Foucault: Reflections on Resistance.* Boston 1988.

Docherty, Thomas: Criticism, History, Foucault. In: *History of*

European Ideas 14 (3). Special Issue [on] Foucault. May 1992, pp. 365–78.

Dover, Kenneth J.: *Greek Homosexuality*. London, 1978.

—— (ed.): Plato: *Symposium*. Cambridge, 1980.

Dreyfus, Hubert Lederer and Rabinow, Paul: *Beyond Structuralism and Hermeneutics*. Chicago, 1982.

Dumézil, Georges: Un Homme Heureux. In: *Le Nouvel Observateur* (1025). Paris, 1984.

During, Simon: *Foucault and Literature: Towards a Genealogy of Writing*. London, New York, 1992.

Engelhardt, Stephan: Michel Foucault, Wahnsinn und Gesellschaft. In: *Philosophisches Jahrbuch* 79 (1972), pp. 219–22.

Erdmann, Eva, et al. (eds.): *Ethos der Moderne: Foucaults Kritik der Aufklärung*. Frankfurt am Main, New York, 1990.

Eribon, Didier: *Michel Foucault*. Paris 1989.

——: *Michel Foucault*. Trans. Betsy Wing. Cambridge, Mass., 1991.

Ewald, François: Foucault verdauen. François Ewald im Gespräch mit Wilhelm Schmid. In: *Spuren (Sonderheft): Michel Foucault. Materialien zum Hamburger Kolloquium* (2–4 December 1988). Hamburg, 1988, pp. 53–6.

Ewald, François and Waldenfels, Bernhard (eds.): *Spiele der Wahrheit: Michel Foucaults Denken*. Frankfurt am Main, 1991.

Faderman, Lillian: *Surpassing the Love of Men*. New York, 1981.

Fernández Liria, Carlos: *Sin Vigilancia y sin Castigo: Una Discusión con Michel Foucault*. Madrid, 1992.

Fink-Eitel, Hinrich: *Foucault zur Einführung*. Hamburg, 1989.

——: *Foucault: An Introduction*. Trans. Edward Dixon. Philadelphia, 1992.

——: Zwischen Nietzsche und Heidegger: Michel Foucaults 'Sexualität und Wahrheit' im Spiegel neuerer Sekundärliteratur. In: *Philosophisches Jahrbuch*. Freiburg, München, 1990, pp. 367–90.

——: Michel Foucaults Analytik der Macht. In: *Die Austreibung des Geistes aus den Geisteswissenschaften*. Paderborn, 1980, pp. 38–78.

Fischer, Gerhard (ed.): Der Staub, der der Wolke trotzt: Michel Foucault. In: *Daedalus – die Erfindung der Gegenwart*. Basel, Frankfurt am Main; 1990, pp. 75–90.

'Florence, Maurice': Foucault, Michel 1926– In: Denis Huisman (ed.), *Dictionnaire des philosophes*. Paris, 1984, pp. 942–4.

Flynn, Thomas R.: Truth and Subjectivation in the later Foucault. In: *The Journal of Philosophy* 82 (1985), pp. 531–40.

——: Foucault as Parrhesiast: His last Course at the Collège de

France (1984). In: *Philosophy and Social Criticism* 12 (1987), pp. 213–76.

Gabbard, David A.: *Silencing Ivan Illich: A Foucauldian Analysis of Intellectual Exclusion*. San Francisco, 1993.

Gane, Mike (ed.): *Towards a Critique of Foucault*. London, New York, 1986.

Goldhill, Simon: *Foucault's Virginity: Ancient Erotic Fiction and the History of Sexuality*. Cambridge, 1995.

Goldstein, Jan (ed.): *Foucault and the Writing of History*. Cambridge, Mass.: Oxford; 1994.

Gordon, Colin (ed.): Michel Foucault: *Power/Knowledge: Selected Interviews and other Writings, 1972–1977*. Brighton, 1980.

——: Question, Ethos, Event: Foucault on Kant and Enlightenment. In: *Economy and Society* 15 (1986), pp. 71–87.

——: The Soul of the Citizen. Max Weber and Michel Foucault on Rationality and Government. In: Scott Lash and Sam Whimster: *Max Weber, Rationality and Modernity*. London, 1987.

Gottschalch, Wilfried: Foucaults Denken – eine Politisierung des Urschreis? In: *Der neue Irrationalismus. Literaturmagazin* 9. Reinbek, 1978, pp. 66–73.

Guilleux, Alain: *Bonheur et Politique chez Michel Foucault*. Paris, 1988.

Gutting, Gary (ed.): *The Cambridge Companion to Foucault*. Cambridge, 1994.

——: *Michel Foucault's Archaeology of Scientific Reason* (Modern European Philosophy). Cambridge, 1989.

Habermas, Jürgen: *Der philosophische Diskurs der Moderne: Zwölf Vorlesungen*. Frankfurt am Main, 1985.

——: *The Philosophical Discourse of Modernity: Twelve Lectures*. Trans. Frederick Lawrence. Cambridge, Mass., 1987.

——: Genealogische Geschichtsschreibung: Über einige Aporien im machttheoretischen Denken Foucaults. In: *Merkur* 38 (1984), pp. 745–53.

——: *Theorie des kommunikativen Handelns*. Frankfurt am Main, 1981.

——: *The Theory of Communicative Action*. Trans. Thomas McCarthy. Boston, 1984.

Halperin, David M.: *Saint Foucault: Towards a Gay Hagiography*. New York, Oxford, 1995.

——: Sexual Ethics and Technologies of the Self in Classical Greece. In: *American Journal of Philosophy* 107 (1986), pp. 274–86.

——: Is there a History of Sexuality? In: *History and Theory* 28 (1989), pp. 257–74.

Harlizius-Klück, Ellen: *Der Platz des Königs: Las Meninas als Tableau des klassischen Wissens bei Michel Foucault.* Wien, 1995.

Hennis, Wilhelm: *Max Webers Fragestellung. Studien zur Biographie des Werks.* Tübingen, 1987.

Hoffmann, Frank: *Genet – Der gebrochene Diskurs. Jean Genets Theater im Licht der Philosophie Michel Foucaults.* Bad Honnef, 1984.

Honegger, Claudia: Michel Foucault und die serielle Geschichte. Über die 'Archäologie des Wissens'. In: *Merkur* 36 (1982), pp. 500–23.

Honneth, Axel: *Kritik der Macht: Reflexionsstufen einer kritischen Gesellschaftstheorie.* Frankfurt am Main, 1985.

Hoy, David Couzens (ed.): *Foucault: A Critical Reader.* Oxford, New York, 1986.

Hunt, Alan and Wickham, Gary: *Foucault and Law. Towards a Sociology of Law as Governance.* London: Boulder, Colo. 1994.

Isenberg, Bo: Habermas on Foucault: Critical Remarks. In: *Acta Sociologica* 34 (1991), pp. 299–308.

Jäger, Christian: Michel Foucault: *Das Ungedachte denken. Eine Untersuchung der Entwicklung und Struktur des kategorischen Zusammenhangs in Foucaults Schriften.* München, 1994.

Kammler, Clemens: *Michel Foucault. Eine kritische Analyse seines Werkes.* Bonn, 1986.

Kamper, Dietmar: Aufklärung – was sonst? In: *Merkur* 436 (1985), pp. 535–40.

Kelly, Michael (ed.): *Critique and Power: Recasting the Foucault/ Habermas Debate.* Cambridge, Mass.; London, 1994.

Kent, Christopher A.: Michel Foucault: Doing History, or undoing it? In: *Canadian Journal of History.* (December 1986), pp. 371–95.

Kittler, Friedrich A. (ed.): *Austreibung des Geistes aus den Geisteswissenschaften: Programme des Poststrukturalismus.* Paderborn, München, Wien, Zürich, 1980.

Koch-Harnack, Gundel: *Knabenliebe und Tiergeschenke – Ihre Bedeutung im päderastischen Erziehungssystem Athens.* Berlin, 1983.

Kögler, Hans-Herbert: *Michel Foucault.* Stuttgart, Weimar, 1994.

Kremer-Marietti, Angèle: *Michel Foucault: Archéologie et Généalogie.* Paris, 1985.

Krieken van, Robert: The Organization of the Soul: Elias and Foucault on discipline and the Self. In: *Archives Européennes de Sociologie* 31 (2) (1990), pp. 353–71.

Künzel, Werner, *Foucault liest Hegel. Versuch einer polemischen Dekonstruktion dialektischen Denkens.* Frankfurt am Main, 1985.

Kusch, Martin: *Foucault's Strata and Fields: An Investigation into Archaeological and Genealogical Science Studies.* Dordrecht, 1991.

Kuster, Martin (ed.): *Entfernte Wahrheit: Von der Endlichkeit der Psychoanalyse.* Tübingen, 1992.

Lanigan, Richard L.: *The Human Science of Communicology. A Phenomenology of Discourse in Foucault and Merleau-Ponty.* Pittsburgh, Penn., 1992.

Lentricchia, Frank: *Ariel and the Police. Michel Foucault, William James, Wallace Stevens.* Madison, Wis., 1988.

Macey, David: *The Lives of Michel Foucault.* London, 1993.

Magiros, Angelika: *Foucaults Beitrag zur Rassismustheorie.* Hamburg, Berlin, 1995.

Mahon, Michael: *Foucault's Nietzschean Genealogy: Truth, Power, and the Subject.* Albany, 1992.

Marques, Marcelo: *Foucault und die Psychoanalyse: Zur Geschichte einer Auseinandersetzung.* Tübingen, 1990.

Marti, Urs: *Michel Foucault.* München, 1988.

Martin, Luther H., et al. (eds.): *Technologies of the Self – A Seminar with Michel Foucault.* Amherst, Mass., 1988.

McHoul, Alec and Grace, Wendy: *A Foucault Primer. Discourse, Power and the Subject.* London, 1995.

McNay, Lois: *Foucault: A Critical Introduction.* Cambridge, Oxford, 1994.

Megill, Allan: *Prophets of Extremity. Nietzsche, Heidegger, Foucault, Derrida.* Berkeley, Los Angeles, London, 1985.

Merquior, José-Guilherme: *Foucault.* London, 1985.

Michel Foucault philosophe: Recontre Internationale (9–11 January 1988). Paris, 1989.

Miguel-Alfonso, Ricardo and Caporale-Bizzini, Silvia (eds.): *Reconstructing Foucault: Essays in the Wake of the 80s.* Amsterdam: Atlanta, Ga.; 1994.

Miller, James: *The Passion of Michel Foucault.* London, 1993.

Minson, Jeffrey: *Genealogies of Morals: Nietzsche, Foucault, Donzelot and the Eccentricity of Ethics.* Basingstoke, 1985.

Morris, Meaghan and Patton, Paul (eds.): *Michel Foucault: Power, Truth, Strategy.* Sydney, 1979.

Natoli, Salvatore: *Ermeneutica e Genealogia: Filosofia e Metodo in Nietzsche, Heidegger, Foucault.* Roma, 1981.

Nehamas, Alexander: *Nietzsche: Life as Literature.* Cambridge. 1985.

———: Nietzsche, Modernity, Aestheticism. In: *Internationale Zeitschrift für Philosophie* 2 (1994), pp. 180–200.

Neuenhaus, Petra: *Max Weber und Michel Foucault: Über Macht und Herrschaft in der Moderne*. Pfaffenweiler, 1993.

Nieraad, Jürgen: Dritte Dimension: Zur Foucault-Darstellung von Gilles Deleuze. In: *Allgemeine Zeitschrift für Philosophie* (1991), pp. 87–93.

Nietzsche, Friedrich: *Sämtliche Werke: Kritische Studienausgabe*. München, Berlin, New York, 1980.

Nordquist, Joan: *Michel Foucault: A Bibliography*. Santa Cruz, Cal., 1986.

O'Farrell, Clare: *Foucault: Historian or Philosopher?* Basingstoke, London, 1989.

Otto, Stephan: *Das Wissen des Ähnlichen. Michel Foucault und die Renaissance*. Frankfurt am Main; Bern; New York; Paris; 1992.

Owen, David: *Maturity and Modernity: Nietzsche, Weber, Foucault and the Ambivalence of Reason*. London, 1994.

Plato: *Symposium*. Trans. Alexander Nehamas and Paul Woodruff. Indianapolis, Ind., 1989.

Poster, Mark: *Foucault, Marxism and History: Mode of Production versus Mode of Information*. Cambridge, 1985.

Prado, C.G.: *Starting with Foucault: An Introduction to Genealogy*. Boulder, San Francisco, Oxford, 1995.

Privitera, Walter: *Stilprobleme: Zur Epistomologie Michel Foucaults*. Frankfurt am Main, 1990.

Prokhoris, Sabine: Die Psychoanalyse, eine Pragmatik des Wahren? Einige Fragen, ausgehend von Michel Foucault. In: Martin Kuster (ed.): *Entfernte Wahrheit: Von der Endlichkeit der Psychoanalyse*. Tübingen, 1992, pp. 85–96.

Puder, Martin: Der böse Blick des Michel Foucault. In: *Neue Rundschau* (1982), pp. 315–24.

Quinby, Lee: *Freedom, Foucault, and the Subject of America*. Boston, Mass., 1991.

Rabinow, Paul (ed.): *The Foucault Reader*. New York, 1984.

Racevskis, Karlis: *Michel Foucault and the Subversion of Intellect*. Ithaca, NY; London; 1983.

Rajchman, John: *Michel Foucault: The Freedom of Philosophy*. New York, 1985.

——: *Truth and Eros: Foucault, Lacan and the Question of Ethics*. New York, 1991.

Ramazanoğlu, Caroline (ed.): *Up Against Foucault: Explorations of some Tensions between Foucault and Feminism*. London, New York, 1993.

Rasmussen, David M. (ed.): *The Final Foucault, Studies on Michel Foucault's Last Works. Philosophy and Social Criticism*, Special Issue. Chestnut Hill, 1987, pp. 110–279.

Reinke-Köberer, Ellen K.: Schwierigkeiten mit Foucault. In: *Psyche* 33 (1979), pp. 364–76.

Reiter, Josef: Der 'endgültige' Tod Gottes. Zum Strukturalismus von Michel Foucault. In: *Salzburger Jahrbuch für Philosophie* 14 (1970), pp. 111–25.

Sawicki, Jana: *Disciplining Foucault: Feminism, Power, and the Body.* New York, 1991.

Schlesier, Renate: Humaniora: Eine Kolumne. In: *Merkur* 38 (1984), pp. 817–23.

Schmid, Wilhelm (ed.): *Denken und Existenz bei Michel Foucault.* Frankfurt am Main, 1991.

———: *Die Geburt der Philosophie im Garten der Lüste: Michel Foucaults Archäologie des platonischen Eros.* Frankfurt am Main 1987.

———: Uns selbst gestalten: Zur Philosophie der Lebenskunst bei Nietzsche. In: *Nietzsche-Studien* 21. Internationales Jahrbuch für die Nietzsche-Forschung (1992), pp. 50–62.

———: Philosophieren über Lebenskunst: Ein Gespräch zwischen Wilhelm Schmid (Berlin/Riga) und Hartwig Schmidt (Berlin). In: *Deutsche Zeitschrift für Philosophie.* (1993), pp. 127–41.

Schneider, Ulrich Johannes: Foucault in Deutschland: Ein Literaturbericht. In: *Allgemeine Zeitschrift für Philosophie* (1991), pp. 71–86.

Schwarz, Richard (ed.): *Zur Genealogie der Regulation: Anschlüsse an Michel Foucault.* Mainz, 1994.

Scott, Charles E.: *The Question of Ethics: Nietzsche, Foucault, Heidegger.* Bloomington, 1990.

Seitter, Walter: Ein Denken im Forschen: Zum Unternehmen einer Analytik bei Michel Foucault. In: Walter Seitter. *Der große Durchblick: Unternehmensanalysen.* Berlin, 1983, pp. 55–97.

———: 'Eine Ethnologie unserer Kultur'. Zum Raum- und Zeitprofil von Foucaults Werk. In: *Spuren (Sonderheft): Michel Foucault.* Materialien zum Hamburger Kolloquium (2–4 December 1988). Hamburg, 1988, pp. 50–2.

Sheridan, Alan: *Michel Foucault: The Will to Truth.* London, 1980.

Shumway, David R.: Michel Foucault. In: *Twayne's World Authors Series: French Literature.* Boston, 1989.

Simons, Jon: *Foucault and the Political: Thinking the Political.* London, New York, 1995.

Slattery, David: *The End of the Anthropological Self. Foucault in the Trobriand Islands.* Poznań, 1993.

Sloterdijk, Peter: Michel Foucaults strukturale Theorie der Geschichte. In: *Philosophisches Jahrbuch* (1972), pp. 161–84.

Smart, Barry: *Foucault, Marxism and Critique.* London, 1985.

——: *Michel Foucault.* London, 1988.

Szakolczai, Arpád: From Governmentality to the Genealogy of Subjectivity: On Foucault's Path in the 1980s. San Domenico (FI) 1993 (EUI Working Papers in Political and Social Sciences No. 93/4).

Veyne, Paul: *Comment on écrit l'histoire suivi de Foucault révolutionne l'histoire.* Paris, 1979.

——: La Fin de Vingt-cinq Siècles de Métaphysique. In: *Le Monde,* 27. June 1984.

Visker, Rudi: *Michel Foucault: Genealogy as Critique.* London, New York, 1995.

Weber, Max: *Science as a Vocation.* Trans. Michael John. In: Peter Lassman and Irving Velody (eds.): *Max Weber's 'Science as a Vocation'.* London, 1989, pp. 3–31.

——: *Political Writings.* eds. Peter Lassman and Ronald Speirs. Cambridge, 1994.

Index

academia, academic, 4, 24, 26, 39,
68, 70, 83–4, 89, 92, 94, 102,
111–12, 126, 132–4, 139, 142
aesthetics of existence, 16–17, 20,
32, 44, 46, 54, 63, 67–8, 71, 76,
79, 83, 85, 100–1, 103, 108–9,
112, 118, 121–2, 124–5, 129, 131,
133, 136, 139
Affairs of the Heart, 57
Alcibiades, 58, 100–1
Alexander, 41, 94–5, 129
agōn, agonistic, agonal, 12, 19, 26–7,
37, 98, 111, 119, 120, 129
amor fati, 39, 121–2
anagkaion, 35–6
anthropological, 33, 66
Antichrist, antichristian, 113,
116–17, 124
anti-hermeneutical (*see also*
hermeneutics), 117, 125
anti-metaphysical (*see also*
metaphysics), 113
antinomy (of the boy), 28, 40, 140
anti-science (*see also* science), 72,
89, 114
aphrodisia, 7–9, 11, 16–19, 25, 27, 29,
30–2, 47–50, 53–4, 56
archaeology, 36, 76, 86, 103
Archaeology of Knowledge, 72
Artemidorus, 33–7, 76
artwork, 19, 79, 83
ascetic(s), 7, 13, 16, 30–1, 33, 44, 56,
59, 100–2, 108, 124–5, 135, 137
asceticism, 12, 83–4, 100, 102, 108,
119
askēsis, 11–14, 94, 100–2, 107–8, 119,
126, 134, 140
attitude (see also critical), 4, 9,
11–12, 14, 16, 18, 20–1, 24, 26–7,
30–1, 33, 37, 40, 43, 46, 56–7, 59,
69, 76, 79–87, 89–95, 98, 101,
115, 126–7, 131–4, 136–7, 140
Aufklärung (*see also* Enlightenment),
69, 132
authenticity, 85, 116
Les Aveux de la Chair, 42, 48, 128

Baudelaire, Charles, 82–5, 87
Bell, Desmond, 70, 78, 102, 131–2,
135
Bernauer, James W., 131
bio-power, 46, 64
bio-politics, bio-political, 80, 105,
110, 138
Birth of the Clinic, 74
Bolz, Norbert, 102, 134–5, 138–9,
141
Boswell, John, 24

Care of the Self, 33, 76, 112, 125
changeability, 66, 71, 116, 126
charis, 56–7
chrēsis, 7, 10–11
chrēsis aphrodision, 10–11
Christianity, (*see also* morality), 3–5,
7–8, 10, 12, 18–19, 30–2, 37,
39–40, 42, 44, 48, 50, 52–54,
59–60, 76, 82, 84–5, 88, 100–1,
111–13, 118–19, 121–2, 124–5,
128, 134–5, 137–9
Christian pastoral, 10, 54, 135, 138
Clark, Michael, 142
coeducation (*see also* education), 27
conduct, 6, 13, 15, 21–2, 26, 29,
31–2, 34, 36, 48, 58, 81, 93,
97–101, 105, 115, 130
individual, 4, 80
masculine, 5, 19

154